THE ALLMAN BROTHERS BAND

CLASSIC MEMORABILIA

1969–1976

This gathering of signed checks and hotel receipts, t-shirts and promo stickers, ticket stubs, and road worn gear is **A TRIBUTE TO A GOLDEN MOMENT IN TIME** when my father strutted proudly and played his heart out every night with his band of brothers. This is the stuff from which history is made.

GALADRIELLE ALLMAN

author of *Please Be with Me: A Song for My Father, Duane Allman*

The Allman Brothers Band is my all-time favorite group and I have collected all of their albums and singles, along with memorabilia that includes stage passes, posters, magazines, and books. **SEEING THE BOOK, I CAN TRULY SAY THAT IT IS EVERYTHING I HAD HOPED FOR AND MORE.** Great photos, many in color, and descriptions, make this a Big House Museum in book form.

MICHAEL BUFFALO SMITH

author of *Rebel Yell: An Oral History of Southern Rock*

Willie Perkins and Jack Weston paint **A VIVID PICTURE OF THE HISTORY OF THE MIGHTY ALLMAN BROTHERS BAND** through the group's memorabilia and gear. These objects come to life through photographs and in-depth tales and tell a story about a band of brothers and their dedicated crew and fans. This book provides a mesmerizing look deep into the lore and history of America's greatest band.

ALAN PAUL

author of *One Way Out: The Inside History of The Allman Brothers Band*

The profound impact The Allman Brothers Band has had on its legions of fans can be distinctly seen by the countless number of avid collectors of memorabilia over the 45 years of the band's history. The music business changed as did the world's technology and now the band has influenced another generation of listeners and collectors. **THIS BOOK SHOWCASES THE PASSION OF COLLECTORS** and those directly connected to one of Rock-n-Roll's greatest bands. Thank you to Jack and Willie for this wonderful collection—your dedication to The Allman Brothers Band continues their legacy.

ROBERT SCHNECK

Executive Director, The Allman Brothers Band Museum at The Big House

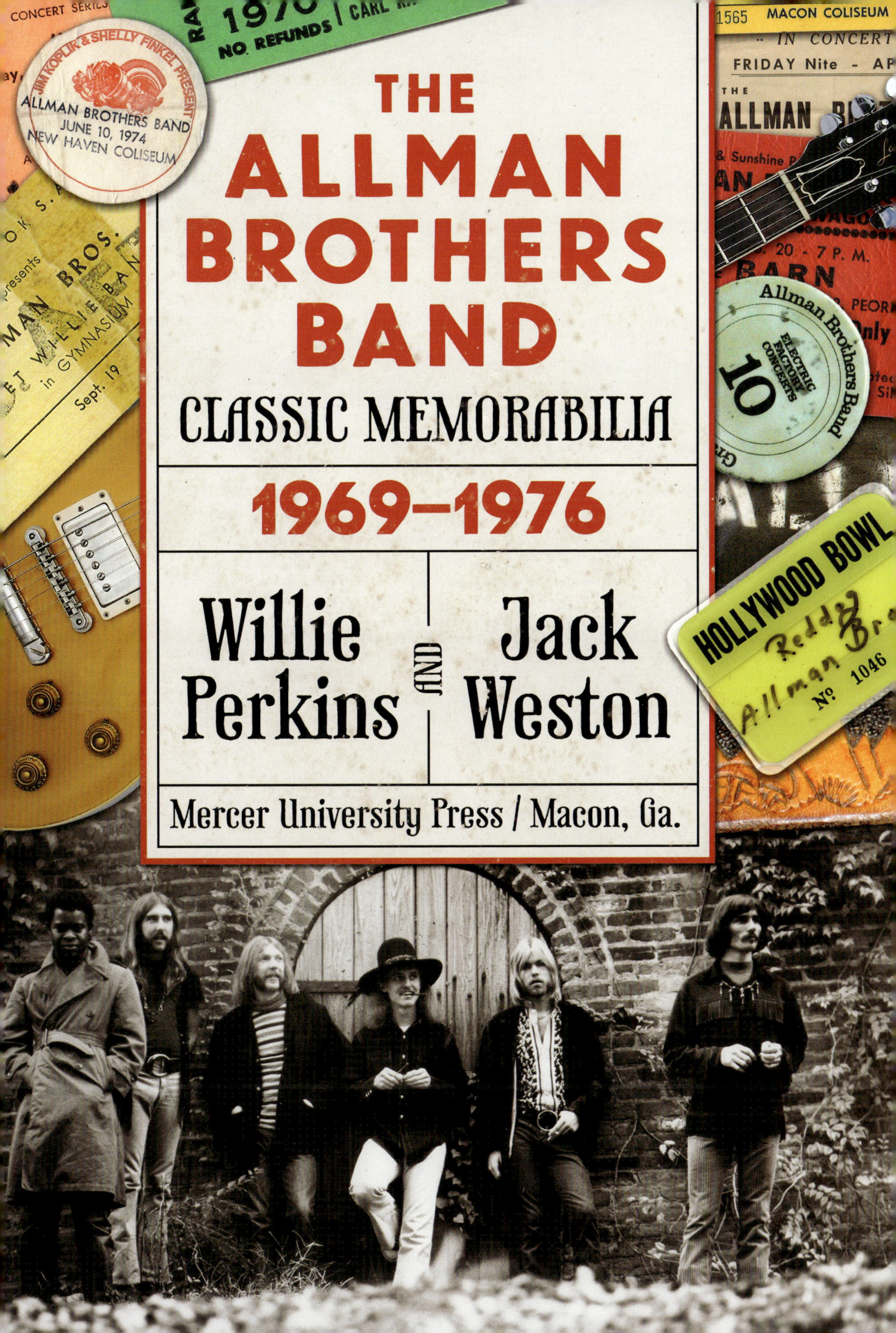

THE ALLMAN BROTHERS BAND
CLASSIC MEMORABILIA
1969–1976
Willie Perkins AND Jack Weston
Mercer University Press / Macon, Ga.
ALLMAN BROTHERS BAND
JUNE 10, 1974
NEW HAVEN COLISEUM
NO REFUNDS
MACON COLISEUM
IN CONCERT
FRIDAY Nite
HOLLYWOOD BOWL
Nº 1046

MUP/ P518

Published by Mercer University Press
1501 Mercer University Drive
Macon, Georgia 31207

9 8 7 6 5 4 3

Books published by Mercer University Press are printed on acid-free paper
that meets the requirements of the American National Standard for Information Sciences—
Permanence of Paper for Printed Library Materials.

Book design by Burt&Burt

ISBN 978-0-88146-547-1

Cataloging-in-Publication Data is available from the Library of Congress

Printed in Canada

To My Friend Sabra
and
Elizabeth LaGrua
Who Really Loved
The Allman Brothers Band

Willie Perkins

To My Wife Connie
and
Daughter Julia

Jack Weston

PREFACE

The Allman Brothers Band was always about the music. From brothers Duane and Gregg Allman's embryonic musical beginnings in 1960's Daytona Beach, Florida, until well into the twenty first century with surviving and newer members, there was never any doubt of that. However, there was a parallel universe of documentation of the band's personal and professional history, much of which survives today.

The Allman Brothers Band was a working band with a backbreaking schedule of touring, songwriting, and recording. There was not a lot of time nor inclination to ponder whether to take a photo, save a pass or ticket stub, grab an advertising poster or keep an old amplifier or instrument but some, both inside and outside the band did, and so a vast universe of Allman Brothers Band items survived and have been preserved over the years.

Allman Brothers Band collector and historian Jack Weston and I have spent hundreds of hours tracing and examining what we consider to be among the rarest and most interesting items of memorabilia of The Allman Brothers Band from both public and private sources. We present them here for historical posterity and our reader's enjoyment.

Willie Perkins
Macon, Georgia

WILLIE PERKINS

I first met and heard The Allman Brothers Band through my longtime friend Twiggs Lyndon who was their original tour manager. He had told me about this extraordinary guitarist Duane Allman and invited me to see and hear the band perform at Atlanta's Piedmont Park. I was immediately mesmerized and knew I had to become a part of their organization. Their music, so powerful and original, was unlike anything I had heard before or since.

The band often stayed at my apartment during their Atlanta visits and we became friends. Through an unusual series of events I became their tour manager in June 1970. I worked with The Allman Brothers Band and Gregg Allman's solo band for about fourteen years and shared with them many of their greatest triumphs and tragedies. I still cherish those memories and the lifelong brotherhood we all shared. The items of memorabilia that exist today are great historical artifacts of those halcyon days of rock and roll.

JACK WESTON

I have been asked how and why I got started collecting Allman Brothers Band memorabilia. It started with my interest in collecting coins, stamps, and baseball cards starting back in the late 1950's and continuing through the mid sixties. During the sixties I was exposed as many of my contemporaries were to various genres of music. When "The Allman Brothers Band at Fillmore East" LP was released in 1971, I was totally hooked. The Allman Brothers Band's music incorporated every type of music I had been exposed to but in a totally different way. It was jazz, blues, folk, country, and rock all combined in a unique package. In the early 1990's I started my subscription to The Allman Brothers Band fanzine *Hittin The Note*. At that time the traders section at the back of each issue had Allman Brothers Band memorabilia for trade. I started trading Allman Brothers memorabilia which included posters, tickets, autographs, passes, and rare concert photos. It did become an obsession for quite some time. For me it was a vehicle to delve into the history of the band as well as to appreciate various graphics from an artistic standpoint. Also it was an opportunity to get to know other Allman Brothers Band memorabilia collectors. The camaraderie with other fans is what I really enjoyed the most. It was referred to among Allman Brothers Band fans as "The Brotherhood." The same brotherhood that started from the band's inception with the original band members, road crew and family. By the end of the 1990's this hobby had evolved to the point where I was buying, selling, trading, and occasionally appraising Allman Brothers Band memorabilia for collectors from around the globe. This book contains some of my most prized Allman Brothers Band items along with artifacts from other collections worldwide.

INTRODUCTION

The late Sixties and early Seventies brought massive cultural changes to America, expressed in music, graphic design, fashion, and literature. A rebellious, outspoken counterculture developed in the long shadow of the war in Vietnam in direct opposition to the conservatism that made that violence possible. A generation of young people found one another by reading signifiers of underground cool: from men's hair grown past their collars to mini skirts and bell bottomed blue jeans. Novels by Vonnegut, Hesse, and Tolkien were carried like talismans, and inspiring music, from folk and rock, to jazz and blues, flowed out of dorm room windows and passing cars. A movement of like minded freaks flew these flags of change proudly.

The Allman Brothers Band has a special place in the history of that time. The Brothers represented the New South, a progressive, creative community largely undiscovered by the larger culture. They brought new fire to the music of the region with an integrated band and looked beyond hip in their wild threads and flowing hair. The band adopted the symbols of the peach and the psychedelic mushroom as their logos, referencing their Georgia home and giving a nod to the drug that inspired their early jams.

My father, Duane Allman, is remembered as an iconic figure. His remarkable playing, his forceful personality, and his hippie style, exemplified by his orange mutton chops, helped define the moment. Because Duane died after less than three years with The Allman Brothers Band, everything connected to that fruitful time is gathered and treasured by collectors.

I have long been fascinated by the avid interest of fans and their hunger for any memento from "the Duane Era." As a child who lost my father, I understand the longing for clues and souvenirs of his life. I once opened a compartment in his guitar case and found a small collection of disposable items that remained there: a sticker from a music shop in New Jersey, a small bar of soap wrapped in wax paper from a Holiday Inn, used guitar strings coiled together, and a few loose picks. These items had an intimate feel the gorgeous guitar itself and the powerful music it made could not convey. Suddenly, my father's traveling life as a musician seemed very real and human. All the material things from his time feel imbued with spirit and meaning now.

I tell my friends in bands to save their schwag. Keep your set lists, backstage passes and posters! I know what they will likely mean to their friends and families in the years to come. But musicians travel at high speed and it falls to the rest of us to gather the swirling remnants left in their wake as a means to tell their stories.

I am grateful to Brother Willie Perkins and collector Jack Weston for pulling together this fascinating collection. Their book charts the growth of The Allman Brothers Band from a grassroots sensation, dependent mostly on word of mouth, to a massive commercial entity. Just as the music evolved and the audience grew, the symbols and signs of the brotherhood also progressed from hand drawn fliers and free shows in Piedmont Park, into an empire of merchandise still sold in venues around the world, forty five years down the road.

This gathering of signed checks and hotel receipts, t-shirts and promo stickers, ticket stubs, and road worn gear is a tribute to a golden moment in time when my father strutted proudly and played his heart out every night with his band of brothers. This is the stuff from which history is made.

Galadrielle Allman

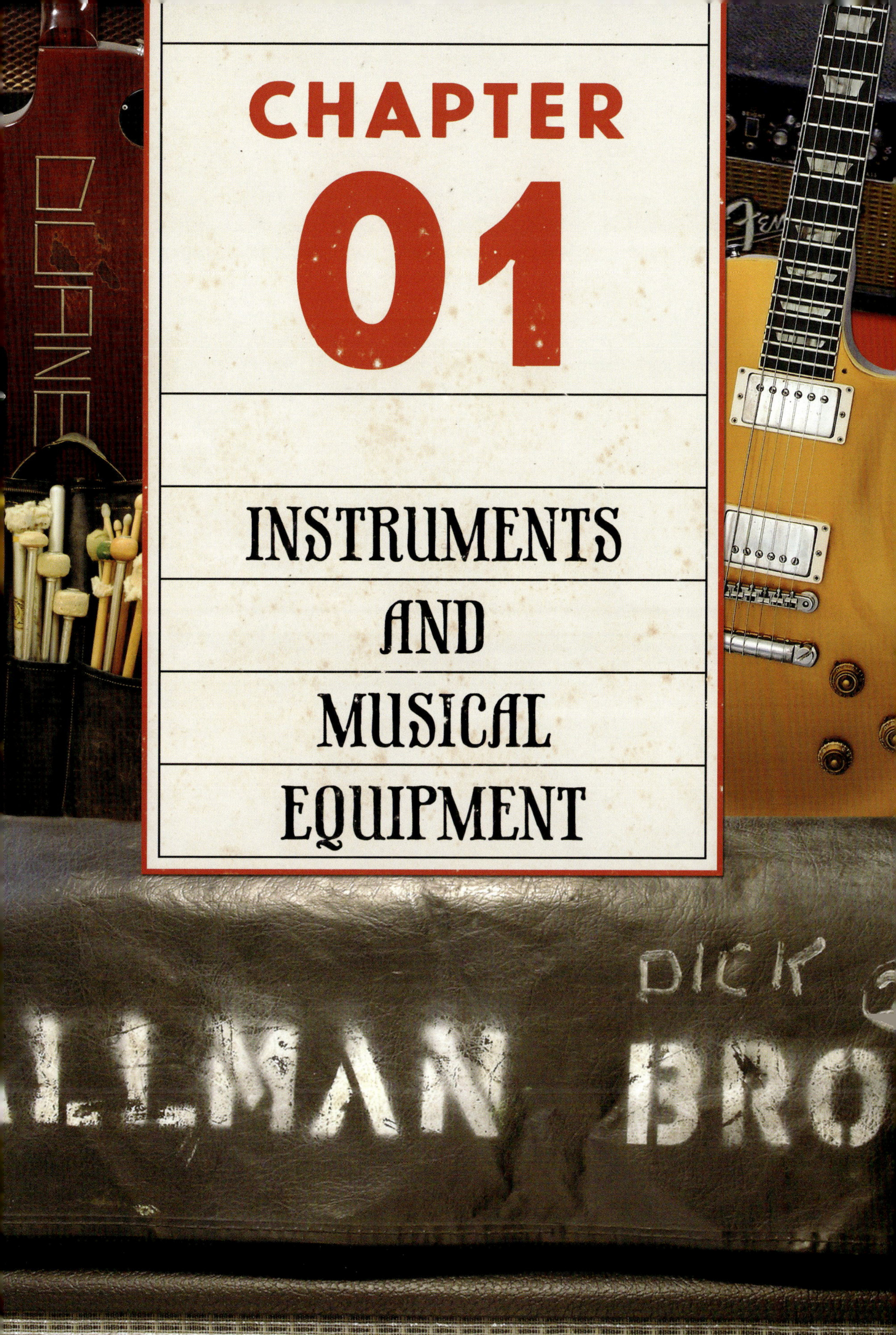

CHAPTER 01

INSTRUMENTS AND MUSICAL EQUIPMENT

OPPOSITE: Dickey Betts' 1968 Fender Bassman amplifier. *Jack Weston collection, Kirk West photo;* **BELOW:** Berry Oakley's and Duane Allman's Fender Showman amplifiers. *Courtesy The Allman Brothers Band Museum at The Big House, Kirk West photo.*

WILLIE PERKINS

The original configuration of The Allman Brothers Band was: Duane Allman: guitars, Gregg Allman: organ and vocals, Dickey Betts: guitars, Berry Oakley: bass guitar, Butch Trucks and Jaimoe: drums and percussion. Chuck Leavell on keyboards and Lamar Williams on bass guitar were additional members of the band during the time frame covered in this book. They joined after the passing of Duane Allman and Berry Oakley.

Their instruments and equipment were the tools of their trade and no concerts or recordings could be made without the instruments, amplifiers, cords, public address sound system, and protective cases. Early on, Buster Lipham of Lipham Music Company in Gainesville, Florida, provided the band a line of credit which enabled them to equip and outfit themselves in a professional manner. The band impressed upon me the importance of making regular payments on their indebtedness to Lipham, but it was often a struggle in those early days. Eventually the debt was retired and future purchases were made in cash or short term financing.

The rigors of touring made short work of standard traveling cases and heavy duty airline type cases were soon required. The band never felt comfortable subjecting their personal stringed instruments to checked baggage or air freight. In early 1971 we were traveling almost exclusively by commercial air and we began purchasing a seat for all of the guitars. This was called "cabin baggage" in airline parlance and was quite unusual. Many a fellow traveler became annoyed when they couldn't get on a full flight because the last seat was taken by a guitar! Later, when the band began using charter aircraft that practice became obsolete.

JACK WESTON

Over the years original band instruments and equipment have become treasured collectibles. Some remain with the original band members or family survivors and others are in public and private collections. I am the owner of a Fender Bassman amplifier (S/N A47466) purchased by The Allman Brothers Band in early 1969 from Lipham Music Company of Gainesville, Florida. It still works perfectly and the vacuum tubes onboard are all vintage. It is a 1968 Fender Silverface Bassman head amplifier and was manufactured in September of 1968. This amplifier was initially used by Duane Allman, Dickey Betts, and Berry Oakley. Eventually it was used as a backup amplifier for Dickey Betts only and designated #3. Twiggs Lyndon wrote #3, Allman Bros. Band, and the name "Dick" in white marker on the back cover of this head amplifier. I also have the original Allman Brothers Band stenciled amplifier cover for Dickey Betts' Fender Bassman amplifier #2 in my collection. Amplifier # 3 was subsequently traded in to Lipham Music Company for Marshall amplifiers and other gear per Buster Lipham. It was then resold by Lipham Music Company to a local church where it remained until 2008. Eventually the amplifier was offered for sale and I purchased it.

A

B

Lipham Music Company, Inc.

1004 N. Main Street • Phone 372-5353
GAINESVILLE, FLORIDA 32601

THE ALLMAN BROTHERS

1 ea.	Gibson ES 345 Serial #540262	$555.00
2 ea.	Bassman tops @ $270.00 ea. Serial #A15619, #A47466	$540.00
1 ea.	used Twin with JBL's Serial #A1049	$605.00
2 ea.	used Dual Showman bottoms @ $475.00 ea. N/A	$950.00
2 ea.	used Dual Showman tops @ $380.00 ea. Serial #A04364,#A03262	$760.00
4 ea.	Marshall speaker cabinets @ $470.00 ea. N/A	$1,880.00
2 ea.	Sunn speaker cabinets @ $795.00 ea. N/A	$1,590.00
16 ea.	12" JBL's @ $105.00 ea N/A	$1,680.00
Payoff to Palus in Jax. on Barry		$518.00
Payoff to Palus in Jax.on Dickie		$256.00
Payoff to Brings & Wilsey on Dickie (in St. Pete)		$130.00
Small goods		$155.00
Hammond B-3, 122 Leslie Cabinet Serial #46113, (Serial #100343) dollies, covers		$3,657.00
Total Retail		$13,276.00
Less trade & Discount		5,844.00
Balance		$7,432.00
State Sales tax		261.12
Total		$7,693.12

C

A Duane Allman's Fender Showman amplifier later owned and used by Ron Blair as a member of Tom Petty and the Heartbreakers. *Courtesy The Allman Brothers Band Museum at The Big House, E. J. Devokaitis Photo.*

B Dickey Betts' Fender Bassman amp cover. Stenciling and handwriting by Twiggs Lyndon in 1969. *Jack Weston collection.*

C Early equipment purchase from 1969 through a line of credit provided by Lipham Music Co. *Courtesy The Allman Brothers Band Museum at The Big House.*

A **TOP:** Rear view Duane Allman's amplifier; **BOTTOM LEFT:** Rear view Berry Oakley's amplifier; **BOTTOM RIGHT:** Front view Dickey Betts' amplifier. *Courtesy The Allman Brothers Band Museum at The Big House, Kirk West photo.*

B Duane Allman's Marshall amplifier with back panel removed showing tubes and electronics. *Courtesy Derek Trucks.*

E

C Front view of Duane Allman's Marshall amplifier now owned and used by Derek Trucks. *Courtesy Derek Trucks.*

D **LEFT:** Rear view of Dickey Betts' amplifier; **RIGHT:** Front view of Duane Allman's amplifier. *Courtesy The Allman Brothers Band Museum at The Big House, Kirk West photo.*

E Rear view of Duane Allman's Marshall amplifier now owned and used by Derek Trucks. *Courtesy Derek Trucks.*

Front view of Duane Allman's late 1950's cherry sunburst Gibson Les Paul guitar.
Courtesy The Rock and Roll Hall of Fame and Museum, owned by Galadrielle Allman.

Back view of Duane Allman's late 1950's cherry sunburst Gibson Les Paul guitar.
Courtesy The Rock and Roll Hall of Fame and Museum, owned by Galadrielle Allman.

Duane Allman's 1957 Gibson Les Paul goldtop guitar. *Courtesy The Allman Brothers Band Museum at The Big House, owned by Scot LaMar, E. J. Devokaitis photo.*

Dickey Betts' Gibson Les Paul Deluxe goldtop guitar with Dickey's and Dan Toler's signatures. *Courtesy The Allman Brothers Band Museum at The Big House, owned by Dr. James Denney, Kirk West photo.*

B

C

A Jaimoe's early drum kit. *Courtesy The Allman Brothers Band Museum at The Big House, Kirk West photo.*

B Jaimoe's drum sticks in case. *Courtesy The Allman Brothers Band Museum at The Big House, Kirk West photo.*

C Butch Truck's drum road case. *Courtesy The Allman Brothers Band Museum at The Big House, Kirk West photo.*

Original band road case also used on "The Allman Brothers Band At Fillmore East" album cover. *Courtesy The Allman Brothers Band Museum at The Big House, Kirk West photo.*

CHAPTER 02

T-SHIRTS

OPPOSITE: President Jimmy Carter wearing "Win, Lose, or Draw" t-shirt. *Courtesy The Allman Brothers Band Museum at The Big House, Kirk West photo.*

WILLIE PERKINS

My earliest recollection of an Allman Brothers Band t-shirt was an advertising and promotional piece issued by the band's record label, Capricorn Records, primarily to the band, their crew members, and Capricorn Records management and staff. The shirt was green in color with the classic Allman Brothers Band mushroom logo imprinted in yellow. The mushroom design was created by artists James Flournoy Holmes and W. David Powell of the Wonder Graphics design studio. They also created The Allman Brothers Band peach truck logo which was used on t-shirts as well. The mushroom design shirt has been reproduced through the years in a variety of styles and colors. It is currently available commercially as a reproduction in the original green and yellow color scheme as well as other color combinations.

I believe the first authorized and commercially available t-shirt was a combination The Allman Brothers Band and Grateful Dead design printed especially for their co-headlining appearance at JFK Stadium in Washington, D.C. on June 09/10, 1973. At about the same time the band members began to realize the commercial value of using their name, likenesses, and images on t-shirts and other merchandise primarily to be sold at concert appearances. Initially, the band planned to administer merchandise sales in-house with assistance from some band members' spouses. This proved to be unwieldy and was soon abandoned. Ultimately, an outside merchandising company, The Great Southern Company, of which I was a shareholder, was retained. The President of Great Southern was Ira Sokoloff, a friend and supporter of the band, who had been active in concert promotion advertising in the New York City metro area. The Great Southern Company paid The Allman Brothers Band cash advances against a royalty percentage on gross merchandise sales. This is the same basis on which recording sales royalties are paid to bands by

'I don't intend to lose'

their record companies. The Great Southern Company manufactured and licensed, with The Allman Brothers Band approval, the distribution and sale of t-shirts, jerseys, and other items including hats, belt buckles, ladies tops, mirrors, pendants, posters, and other items. The greatest percentage of income always came from direct sales of t-shirts at concert events. The Allman Brothers Band sometimes required concert promoters to manufacture about three dozen event specific t-shirts for the band and promoter only. These usually contained a band logo on the front and event specifics on the reverse. Also, some concert promoters on their own created limited edition event specific shirts. Often they were of very high quality with intricate designs.

Bootleg and counterfeit t-shirts were a major problem. Bootlegs contained an unauthorized design and use of The Allman Brothers Band name. Counterfeits were an attempt to copy an existing band design such as the mushroom logo. These shirts were usually imported, and the quality of printing and design was substandard. They were sold primarily in metro areas on street corners adjacent to the concert venue by devious thieves who employed teams of young people to handle the actual sales. Needless to say, they paid the band nothing and the fan got an inferior product. It was outright thievery and a fraud on band fans. The Great Southern Company was able to go into Federal Court in many of these major metro markets and get cease and desist and restraining orders against both known and "John Doe" infringers under United States copyright laws. United States Marshals would hit the streets around the venue and seize bogus merchandise and cash from the offenders like a drug bust. It was expensive, but usually cost effective. I was always pleased to see these thieves stopped in their tracks, but like cockroaches they popped up over and over again. All major bands and solo artists have had to deal with this problem but I always supported strong efforts to protect The Allman Brothers Band and their fans from these unscrupulous outsiders.

OPPOSITE: Original limited production mushroom t-shirt made for band, crew, and record company employees. *Courtesy The Allman Brothers Band Museum at The Big House, Kirk West photo.*

JACK WESTON

My favorite and most prized Allman Brothers Band t-shirts are of the very early 1970's classic mushroom design. The 1970 green with yellow imprint and 1971 orange with white imprint are favorites. In 1973 the multi-colored ABB classic mushroom t-shirt was produced by Great Southern Company on various colored t-shirts. This version is also a highly sought after Allman Brothers Band t-shirt among collectors. The Great Southern 1972 "Eat A Peach" logo on a tan t-shirt is another example I really like. High grade examples of these classic t-shirts from the early 1970's are rare and highly sought after by ABB memorabilia collectors. Most of these were obtained at shows but some were also purchased by mail in a response to ads in The ABB tour program. A 1970 green with yellow classic mushroom imprint in near mint condition would be among the most highly treasured t-shirts by collectors.

Second series "Mushroom" t-shirt. *Jack Weston collection.*

"Mushroom" t-shirt sold to the public by Great Southern Company. *Jack Weston collection.*

ABOVE: "Mushroom" baseball jersey sold to the public by Great Southern Company, *Jack Weston collection;* **BELOW:** "Warehouse New Orleans" shirt given to all bands and road crews performing there. *Courtesy The Allman Brothers Band Museum at The Big House, Kirk West photo.*

"Eat A Peach" t-shirt sold to the public by Great Southern Company. *Jack Weston collection.*

"Mushroom" t-shirt produced by promoter Leas Campbell for band and road crew.
Courtesy The Allman Brothers Band Museum at The Big House, Kirk West photo.

ABOVE: Peach logo, "Brothers and Sisters" t-shirt, circa 1973. *Jack Weston collection;* **BELOW:** Back view of limited edition event t-shirt produced for band and road crew. This venue was at one time named in honor of Duane Allman. *Courtesy The Allman Brothers Band Museum at The Big House, Kirk West photo.*

ABOVE: Front of limited edition event t-shirt produced for band and road crew. *Courtesy The Allman Brothers Band Museum at The Big House, Kirk West photo;* **BELOW:** Front of Willie Perkins' personal "Win, Lose, or Draw" tour jersey. *Jack Weston collection.*

Back of Willie Perkins' personal "Win, Lose, or Draw" tour jersey. *Jack Weston collection.*

"Win, Lose, or Draw" t-shirt sold to the public by Great Southern Company. *Jack Weston collection.*

"Tour 75" t-shirt sold to the public by Great Southern Company, 1975. *Courtesy The Allman Brothers Band Museum at The Big House, Kirk West photo.*

CHAPTER 03

PASSES

OPPOSITE: Very early pinback stage pass used by road crew that proved impractical. *Jack Weston collection.*

WILLIE PERKINS

"It's ok, I'm with the band!" That hackneyed phrase lampooning the efforts of unauthorized persons to gain access to the concert venue and/or backstage area became so prevalent it inspired a well known t-shirt with that inscription.

Early on there was very little effort by The Allman Brothers Band to control access to the concert venue or backstage area. The typical early 1970's concert venue security consisted of a controlled general admission area accessed by a printed ticket. The stage door entrance for band and crew was usually manned by a lone promoter representative with another at the internal entrance to the backstage area. The Allman Brothers Band was notorious for granting complimentary admission to their fans and allowing them onstage. It became somewhat of a tradition and there was little band interest in restricting guests. At some point it did become a financial and safety issue. Promoters were the first to attempt some form of control by issuing their own simple passes usually of the paper or satin cloth peel-and-stick variety.

Eventually The Allman Brothers Band began developing their own internally produced passes. There was much experimentation and a few false starts. Some stick on type passes were easily removed and transferred to others. Early experiments included pin on types which also proved unwieldy. Eventually a system evolved using a permanent pass for band members, crew, and family. The most successful of these was a blue plastic disc about the size of a beverage coaster. It was embossed with the classic mushroom design and contained a small opening for attachment to a lanyard or belt loop. Most band members either lost them or didn't use them. They were easily recognized and rarely left the backstage area once inside the venue. A typical band guest received a complimentary ticket which entitled them to general admission and a reserved seat where applicable. Additional guest passes are largely self explanatory: backstage, backstage after show, or the most coveted, all area access. These were of the satin cloth stick on type in a variety of designs and colors. Some were themed to a particular

THE ALLMAN BROS. BAND

STAGE PASS

tour. By the mid 1970's the band had a printed chart illustrating the various types of authorized passes which the production manager would explain to venue security personnel on the day of the performance. Some promoters had their own passes for particular events, but The Allman Brothers Band passes were usually still used and superseded all others. By the early 1980's most security passes were of rectangular laminated plastic on lanyards, but those are beyond the scope of this book.

JACK WESTON

The first experimental Allman Brothers Band tour pass was a red plastic badge with a pin attachment. This pass had "The Allman Bros. Band Stage Pass" embossed on it. It looked similar to convention passes at the time. These early passes were not used very long by The Allman Brothers Band road crew as they were hard to put on and remove with a very cumbersome pin attached to the back. In 1972 The Allman Brothers Band started to employ stick on satin passes that were produced by the Fasson and Starliner companies. These firms were the primary suppliers of passes to the band during the early to mid 1970's. My favorite early 1970's Allman Brothers Band pass is a 1972 white satin crew pass which has an Allman Brothers Band classic mushroom imprint. This rare pass was produced by the Starliner Company. In January of 1974 an Allman Brothers Band security sheet was conceived by Twiggs Lyndon to distribute to venues and promoters. It was a color 8 x 10 Kodak photo print with January 1974 printed on the back. All of the various Allman Brothers Band classic mushroom passes available at that time are shown on this sheet. The passes were stage crew only, stage access guest, backstage only, and a blue plastic stage crew pass. In 1975, The Allman Brothers Band used the "Win, Lose, or Draw" playing card design. This design was originally conceived by Twiggs Lyndon for the "Win, Lose, or Draw" LP. These passes were used for back stage only access. The pass design incorporated the LP motif with an Ace of mushrooms and Ace of peaches playing cards. The colors were red, green, blue, and black. The companies that produced these passes were MACbak and Fasson.

A

B

C

A Early stick-on stage crew pass used by band crew. *Jack Weston collection.*

B Early stick-on stage crew only used by band crew. *Courtesy The Allman Brothers Band Museum at The Big House, E. J. Devokaitis photo.*

C Three early stick-on back stage passes. *Courtesy The Allman Brothers Band Museum at The Big House, Kirk West photo.*

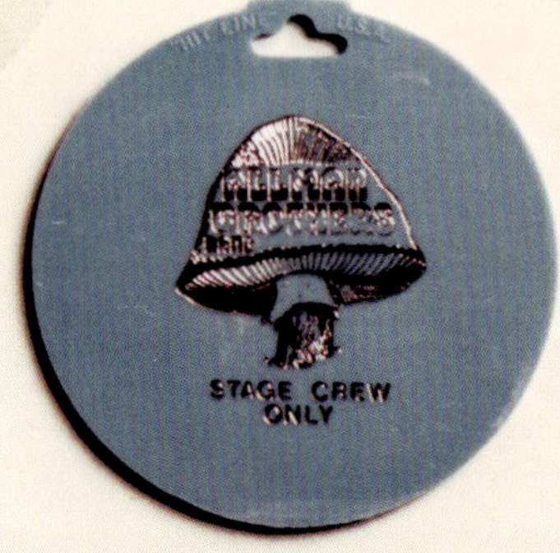

THE ABOVE THREE PASSES ENTITLES THE BEARER TO FREE ACCESS OF THE STAGE, THE DRESSING ROOMS AND THE BACKSTAGE AREA.

THE ABOVE "BACK STAGE ONLY" PASS DOES NOT ENTITLE THE BEARER TO ACCESS OF THE STAGE OR THE DRESSING ROOMS, BUT IS LIMITED TO ACCESS OF THE BACK STAGE AREA ONLY.

Internal 8 x 10 color photo sheet showing various passes prepared by Twiggs Lyndon for production meeting use, circa 1974. *Jack Weston collection.*

A

B

C

A Two early stick on passes. *Jack Weston collection.*

B Very early and rare stick on crew pass. *Jack Weston collection.*

C Event pinbacks from "Mar Y Sol" festival held in Puerto Rico, circa 1972. *Jack Weston collection.*

ABOVE: Event Performer pinback from Mar Y Sol festival with 18K original Allman Brothers Band mushroom pendant. *Jack Weston collection;* **BELOW:** Laminated crew pass for Red Dog from Hollywood Bowl, circa 1972. *David Schless collection.*

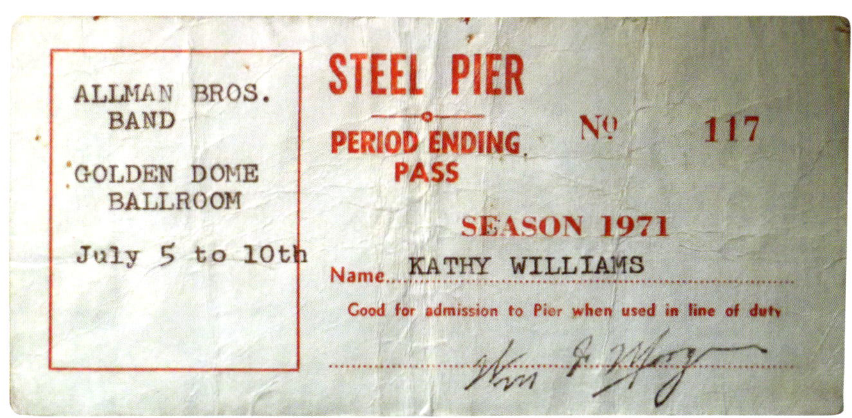

ABOVE: Guest pass, Steel Pier Atlantic City, New Jersey, circa 1971. *David Schless collection;* **BELOW:** Artist event pinback, Macon, Georgia, charity benefit, circa 1975. *Jack Weston collection.*

A

B

C

D

A Event stick-on pass for New Haven Coliseum, circa 1974. *Jack Weston collection.*

B *(left)* Grateful Dead event artist/crew pinback pass JFK stadium, June 9, 1973: *(right)* The Allman Brothers Band event artist/crew pinback pass JFK stadium, June 10, 1973. *Courtesy Grateful Dead Productions/Rhino Entertainment, Jack Weston collection.*

C Rare embossed plastic disc stage pass worn on belt loop, circa 1973–1976. *Jack Weston collection.*

D Event band and crew pinback pass for Watkins Glen, circa July 1973. *Jack Weston collection.*

A

B

ABOVE: Promoter all area access passes for Wakins Glen Summer Jam festival. *Jack Weston collection;* **BELOW:** "Win, Lose, or Draw" stick-on tour passes, circa 1975. *Jack Weston collection.*

ABOVE: Event stick-on pass, Superdome grand opening concert, circa 1975. *Jack Weston collection;* **BELOW:** Event card stock backstage pass, Superdome grand opening concert, circa 1975. *David Schless collection.*

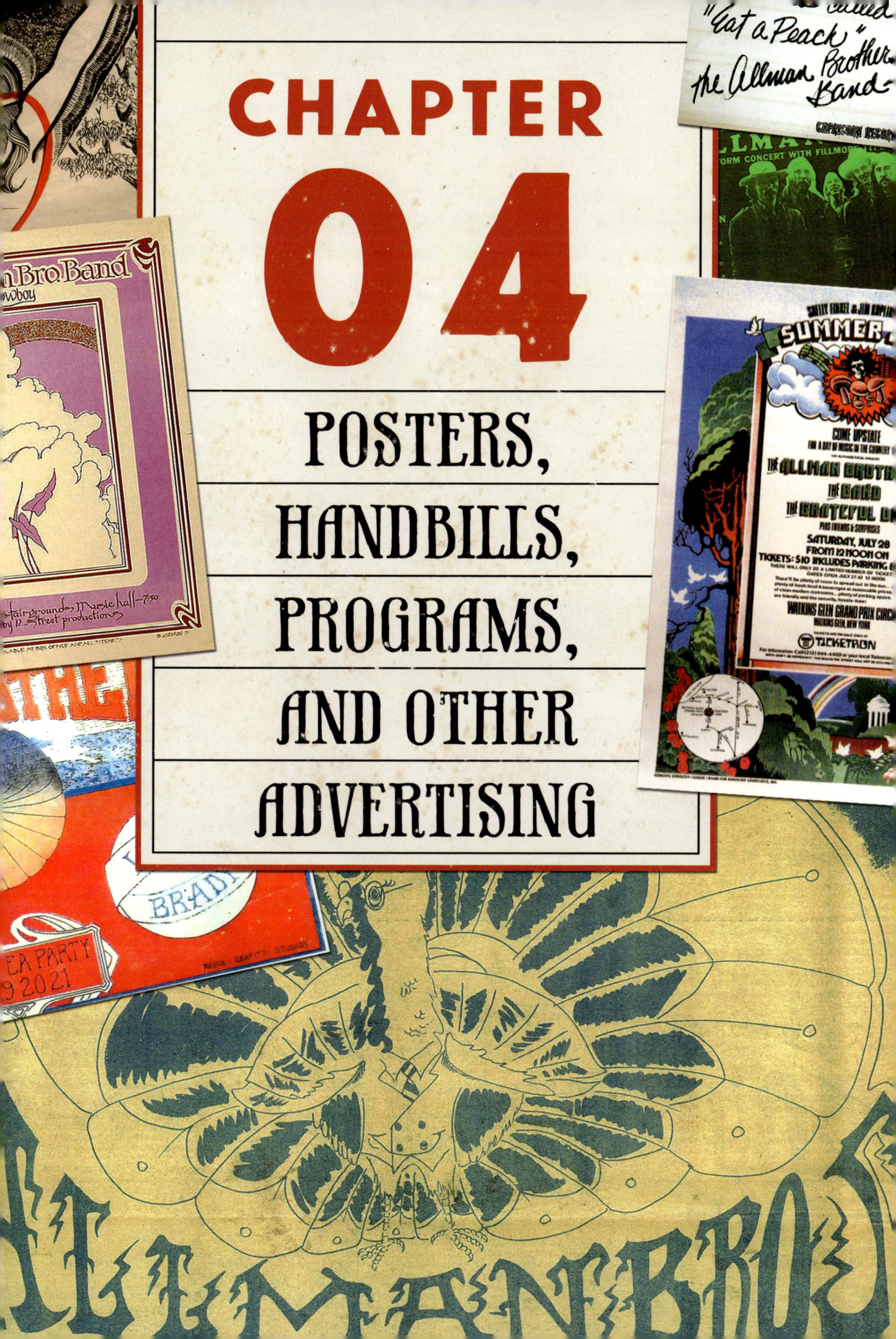

CHAPTER 04

POSTERS, HANDBILLS, PROGRAMS, AND OTHER ADVERTISING

WILLIE PERKINS

The Allman Brothers Band rarely saw much advertising or promotional material for their concert appearances. The band arrived in town on the day of the show or sometimes the night before. After performing the concert they were off to the next event. Early concert advertising posters were predominately displayed on utility poles or in store windows. They were produced entirely at the expense and discretion of the concert promoter. Some would use photographic images of the band members and the name of the band. Handbills and flyers were smaller versions of posters or some variation of them. They were literally handed out to the public or placed on automobile windshields. All posters and handbills contained the date, time, and location of the event along with ticket prices and the names of all performing bands. Some were elaborately designed and in ornate script while others were in simple block printing. As The Allman Brothers Band career progressed their management was able to demand that they receive 100% top headline billing with no other print larger than that used for the band name. In instances where other bands of equal stature jointly appeared, The Allman Brothers Band management demanded alphabetical listing from top left. This would almost automatically guarantee them the premier spot in all advertising.

Many concerts of the mid to late 1960's through the 1970's were advertised in local print media collectively known as the alternative or underground press. Some well remembered examples include *The Great Speckled Bird* in Atlanta, *The Village Voice* in New York City, *The L. A. Free Press* in Los Angeles, and *The Boston Phoenix* among others. It was always a treat for The Allman Brothers Band to arrive in New York and see a huge, full page ad for their upcoming concerts there in *The Village Voice*. Some promoters also advertised in traditional daily newspapers to a lesser extent.

On rare occasions promoters might prepare an event souvenir program for concertgoers at large events or festivals. As The Allman Brothers Band achieved stardom their merchandisers printed and sold tour specific programs. These programs contained photos, short articles, tour itineraries and other items of interest to their fans.

None of the items discussed, other than perhaps programs, were designed to be saved. Most were quickly discarded. Rare and interesting examples of surviving items in good or pristine condition are highly desirable among fans and collectors today.

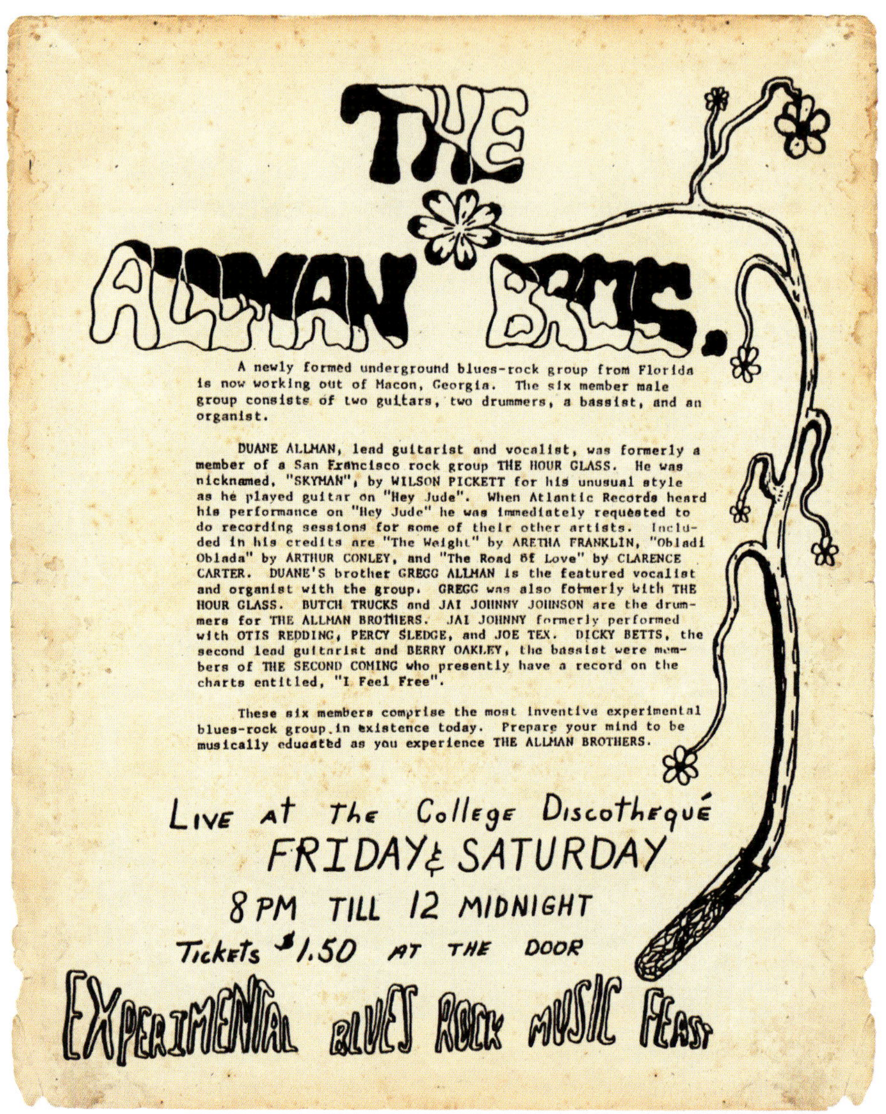

Flyer for the first Allman Brothers Band paid concerts in Macon, May 2-3, 1969. Twiggs Lyndon did a voiceover radio commercial for this show. *Courtesy The Allman Brothers Band Museum at The Big House*

JACK WESTON

My favorite collectibles of The Allman Brothers Band have been paper items, posters, handbills, ads, and programs in particular. These items being ephemera were typically produced to dispose of shortly after they were used, relegating many to the trash bin years ago. The hunt for high grade examples keeps me on the lookout—online auctions, networking, trades, or whatever it takes—to come up with another fine example. Allman Brothers Band posters and handbills from 1969-1971 are the most coveted because they were produced during Duane Allman's lifetime. As a result they command the highest prices among collectors.

Posters and handbills sometimes include images from the band's publicity photos. Jim Marshall and Stephen Paley publicity photos were the most used images for the early posters, handbills, and ads. Intricate designs were also employed using Art Nouveau and many other artistic styles. Printing methods were wood block, offset, lithography, and even photocopies. The first Allman Brothers Band handbill was for the College Discotheque concerts in Macon, Georgia, on May 2 and 3, 1969. This handbill was created using a typed 8 x 10 sheet of paper. Then a flower coming out of what appears to be a test tube was hand drawn on the sheet. At the bottom of the handbill "Experimental Blues Rock Feast" was typed. This handbill says it all "Prepare your mind to be musically educated as you experience The Allman Brothers." This handbill was ahead of its time and so was The Allman Brothers Band.

Proper conservation techniques are necessary to protect and preserve paper items which in many cases are irreplaceable. All paper items in my collection are contained in Mylar conservation sleeves to protect them from contamination and fingerprints. As some of these items were originally printed on paper that was not acid free, they need to be separated so the acid will not migrate from one paper artifact to another. I have used Lineco Neutral pH adhesive to make minor repairs on posters and handbills with great success. These items can be cleaned occasionally if needed with a product called Groomstick paper cleaner. If in doubt on how to proceed with conservation or repairs always contact a professional conservator for rare and valuable items.

ABOVE: Poster from early Florida concert, 1969. *Courtesy The Allman Brothers Band Museum at The Big House;* **OPPOSITE:** Poster from early Atlanta concert, 1969. *Jack Weston collection.*

TURKEY TRIP
ALLMAN BROS.
HAMPTON GREASE BAND
BRICK WALL
SWEET YOUNG'UNS
BOOGER BAND
ADVANCED TICKET SALES
Atlantis Rising
Music City—Ansley Mall
Melody Music—
Greenbrier Shopping Center
Tape City—Rosewell Rd.
SPECIAL GUEST?!!!...
ISN'T THAT INSIDIOUS!
LIGHTS BY ELECTRIC COLLAGE
NOV. 22 SATURDAY
NOV. 23 SUNDAY
ADMISSION 3.00 PER DAY
Duke TIRE CO.
WAREHOUSE
MITCHELL & ELLIOT
PRODUCED BY ATLANTIS RISING PRODUCTIONS
GEMINI PRODUCTIONS © 1969

The RAPP
Pensacola Beach, Fla.
Presents
THE ALLMAN
BROTHERS
Fri. - Sat. - Sun.
AUG. 28, 29, 30
Jam with the Allman Bros.
Sunday - 3:00 to 6:00 p.m.

August 1970 concerts. The band had just met Eric Clapton in Miami during the "Layla" sessions. *Courtesy The Allman Brothers Band Museum at The Big House.*

Rare and highly collectible 1970 concert poster. *Courtesy The Allman Brothers Band Museum at The Big House, Twiggs Lyndon photo.*

ABOVE: Ultra rare 1970 handbill. *Courtesy The Allman Brothers Band Museum at The Big House, Stephen Paley photo;* **BELOW:** November 1970 poster from promoter Don Law's Boston Tea Party Ballroom. *Courtesy The Allman Brothers Band Museum at The Big House, Kirk West photo.*

-- IN CONCERT --

FRIDAY Nite - APRIL 9

THE

ALLMAN BROTHERS

BAND

ADVANCE
TICKETS
$3.
$4.
$5.
AT
Coliseum
BOX OFFICE
Disc-O-Tape

TICKETS BY MAIL
Do it NOW!!
Send Money Orders only, with a self-addressed, stamped envelope to:
ALLMAN BROS. CONCERT
200 Coliseum Drive
Macon, Ga.

Jai Johanny, Berry Oakley, Duane Allman, Butch Trucks, Greg Allman, Dickie Betts

PLUS

COWBOY

AT

MACON COLISEUM

Show Time 8:00 P. M.

Talent Supplied By

Jet Set Enterprises, Inc. Promotions

RIGHTEOUS NAME IN ENTERTAINMENT

Phone (904) 398-3786 4167 San Jose Blvd. (Suite 2) Jacksonville, Fla. 32207

One of the many pairings with Cowboy as the opening act. *Courtesy The Allman Brothers Band Museum at The Big House, Twiggs Lyndon photo.*

ABOVE: Rare, highly collectible 1971 poster. *Courtesy The Allman Brothers Band Museum at The Big House, Twiggs Lyndon photo;* **BELOW:** One of Duane Allman's last concerts. *Courtesy The Allman Brothers Band Museum at The Big House.*

ABOVE: This poster design, with original artwork by Bill Narum, was used for Houston, Dallas, and Austin 1971 concerts. *Courtesy Nico Narum, Kirk West collection;* **BELOW:** University of California concert from October 1971—this was Duane Allman's last west coast performance.

Beautiful art deco designed handbill from 1972. *Courtesy Steve Winwood, Jack Weston collection.*

Rare, early 1972 handbill. This was the first headline show in Macon after Duane Allman's death. *Jack Weston collection.*

SUNSET RUSH
PRODUCTION
MARCH 27
8 P.M.
ALLMAN
BROS. BAND
ALEX TAYLOR
W/ FRIENDS & NEIGHBORS
PERSHING AUD. LINCOLN, NEBR.
TICKETS: $4.50 (ADV.) AT BRANDEIS, CHESSKING &
PERSHING, 5.00 AT DOOR. NO RES. SEATS.
ART BY STEAMBOAT FOR ZERO Graphics...

ABOVE: 1972 handbill; **BELOW:** 1972 handbill. Chuck Leavell was a member of Dr. John's band at this time. *Jack Weston collection;* **OPPOSITE:** Handbill from March 1972. Chuck Leavell was a member of Alex Taylor's band at this time. *Jack Weston collection.*

Watkins Glen, 1973 poster. *Courtesy Grateful Dead Productions/Rhino, Kirk West collection.*

TONY RUFFINO, LARRY VAUGHN & DON LAW

present

THE ALLMAN BROTHERS BAND

TUES. NOVEMBER 25 at 8 P.M.

PROVIDENCE CIVIC CENTER

Tickets $6.50 Advance $7.50 Day of Show

PAID FOR BY THE COMMITTEE FOR JIMMY CARTER. R.J. LIPSHULTZ—TREAS.
TICKET PURCHASE IS A CONTRIBUTION TO THE JIMMY CARTER PRESIDENTIAL CAMPAIGN.

A COPY OF OUR REPORT IS FILED WITH THE FEDERAL ELECTION COMMISSION, WASHINGTON, D.C.

1975 poster. First in a series of benefit concerts for Jimmy Carter. *Kirk West collection.*

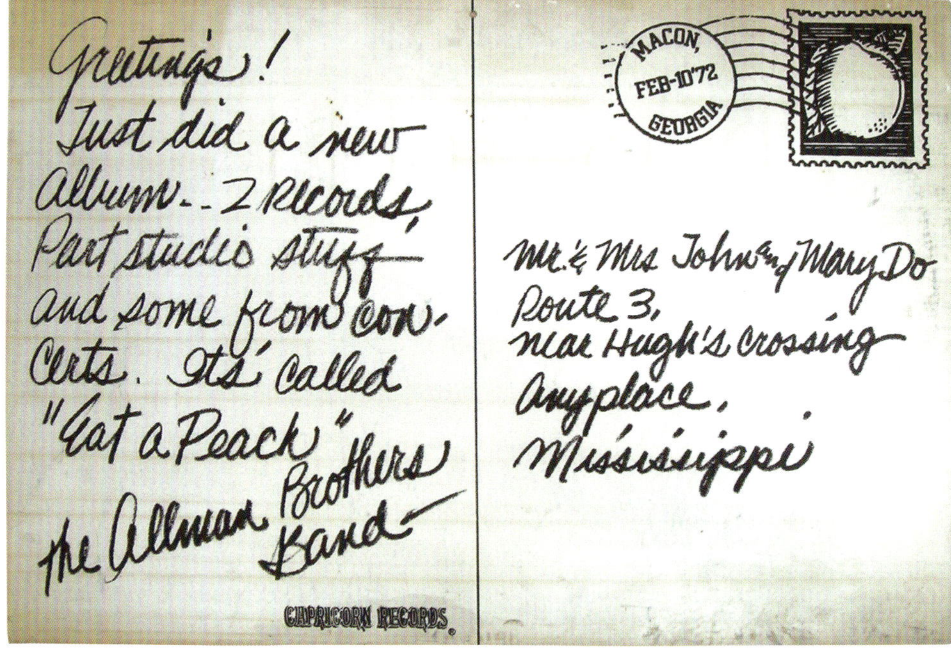

Jumbo promotional postcard (front and back) from Capricorn Records.
Jack Weston collection.

Promotional poster from 1972. The photo was taken at James Arness' ranch.
Jack Weston collection, Twiggs Lyndon photo.

SOUVENIR PROGRAM
1970 LOVE VALLEY ROCK FESTIVAL
25¢
The Love Valley Thing

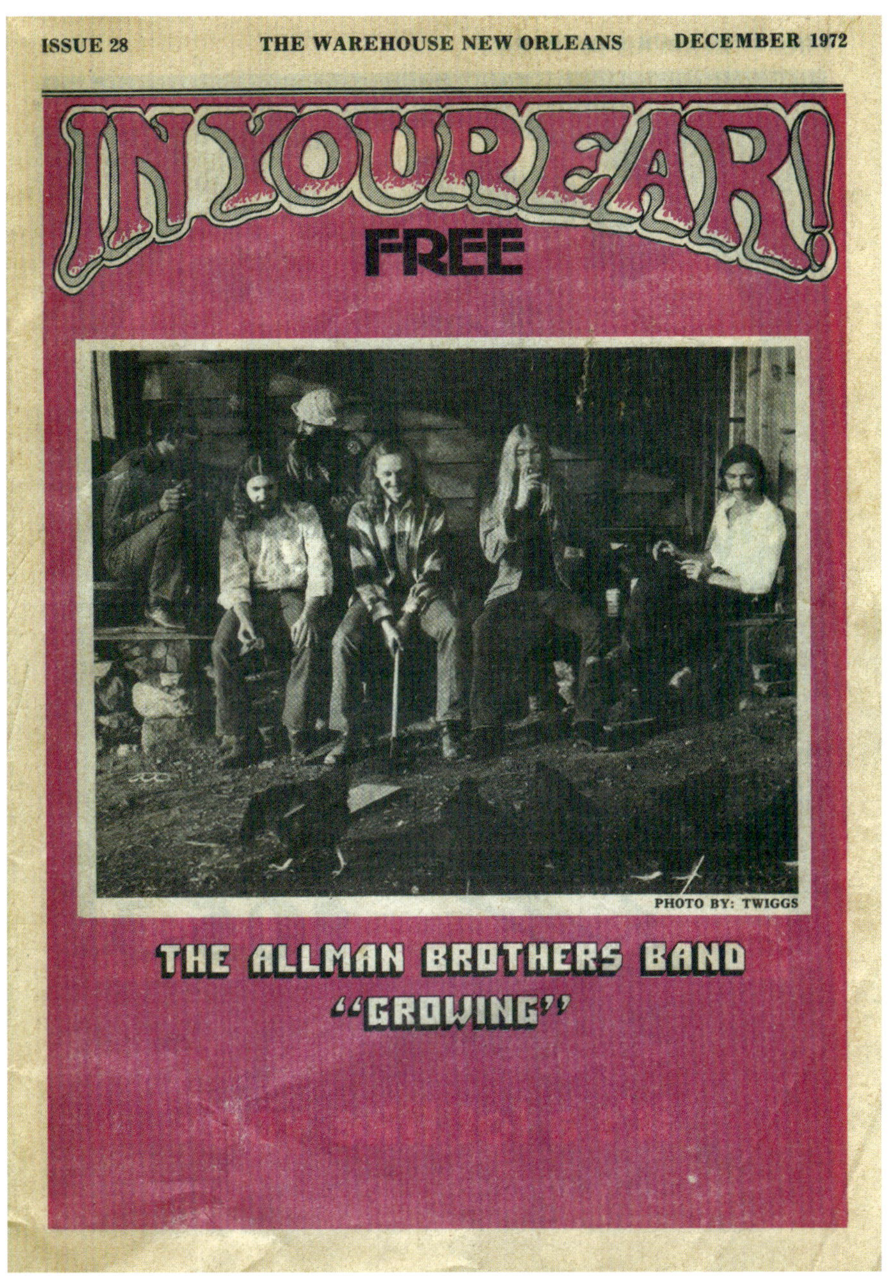

ABOVE: "The Warehouse" concert program with a feature article on The Allman Brothers Band, 1972. *Courtesy The Allman Brothers Band Museum at The Big House,*
OPPOSITE: Program from Love Valley Festival, 1970. A multi-day event headlined by The Allman Brothers Band. *Courtesy The Allman Brothers Band Museum at The Big House.*

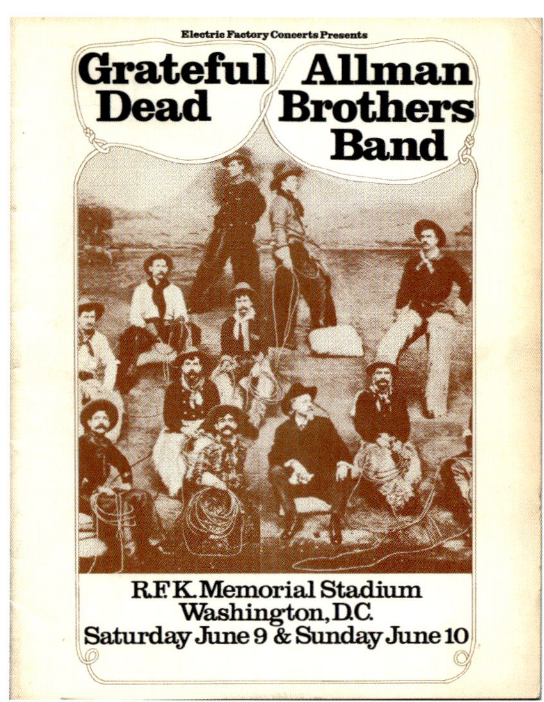

ABOVE: Souvenir program Hollywood Bowl, 1972. *Jack Weston collection;* **BELOW:** A souvenir program from June 1973 for RFK stadium, Washington D.C., *Courtesy Grateful Dead Productions/Rhino, Jack Weston collection.*

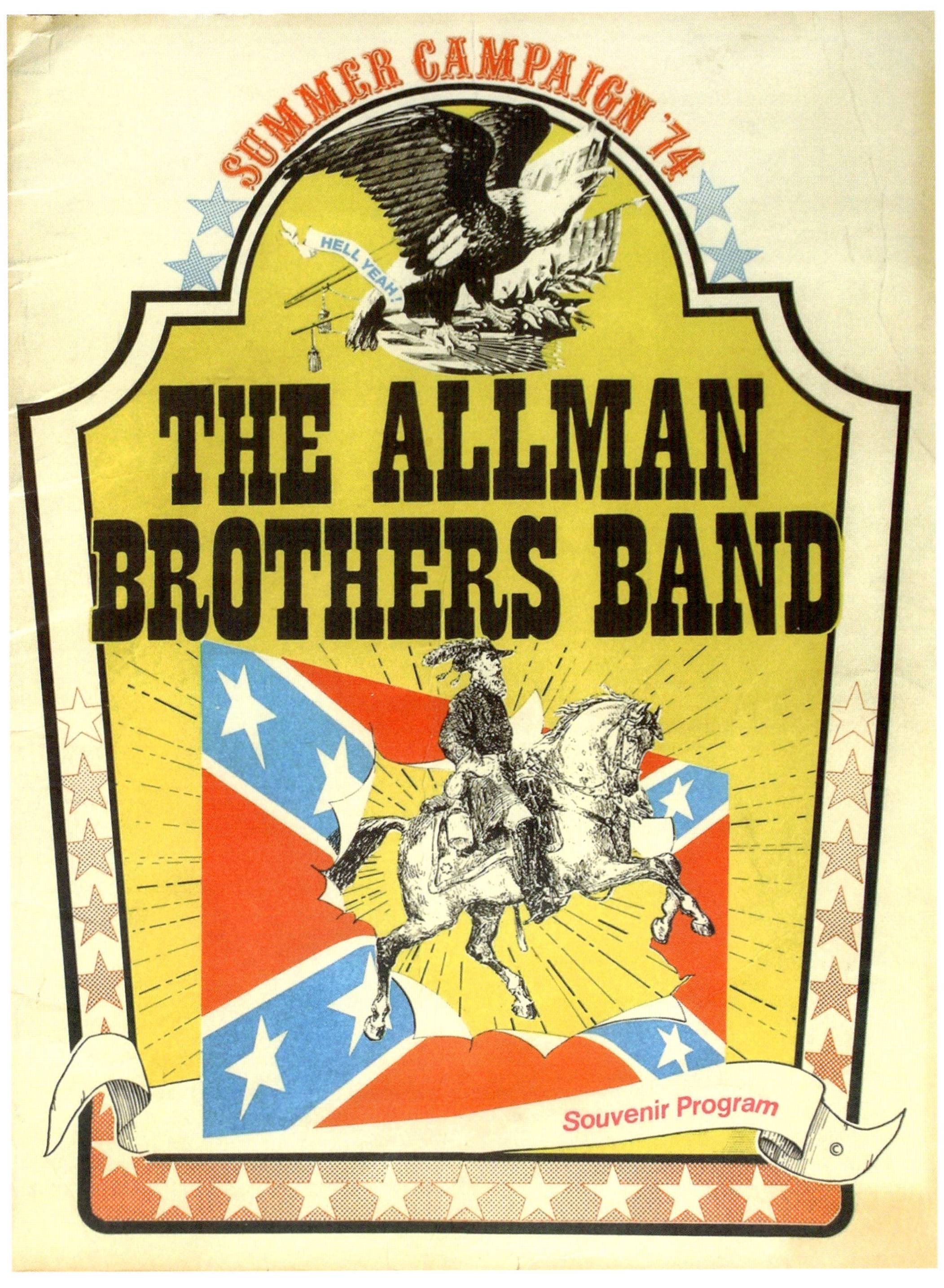

1974 tour souvenir program sold by The Great Southern Company. *Jack Weston collection.*

1975 tour souvenir program sold by The Great Southern Company. *Jack Weston collection.*

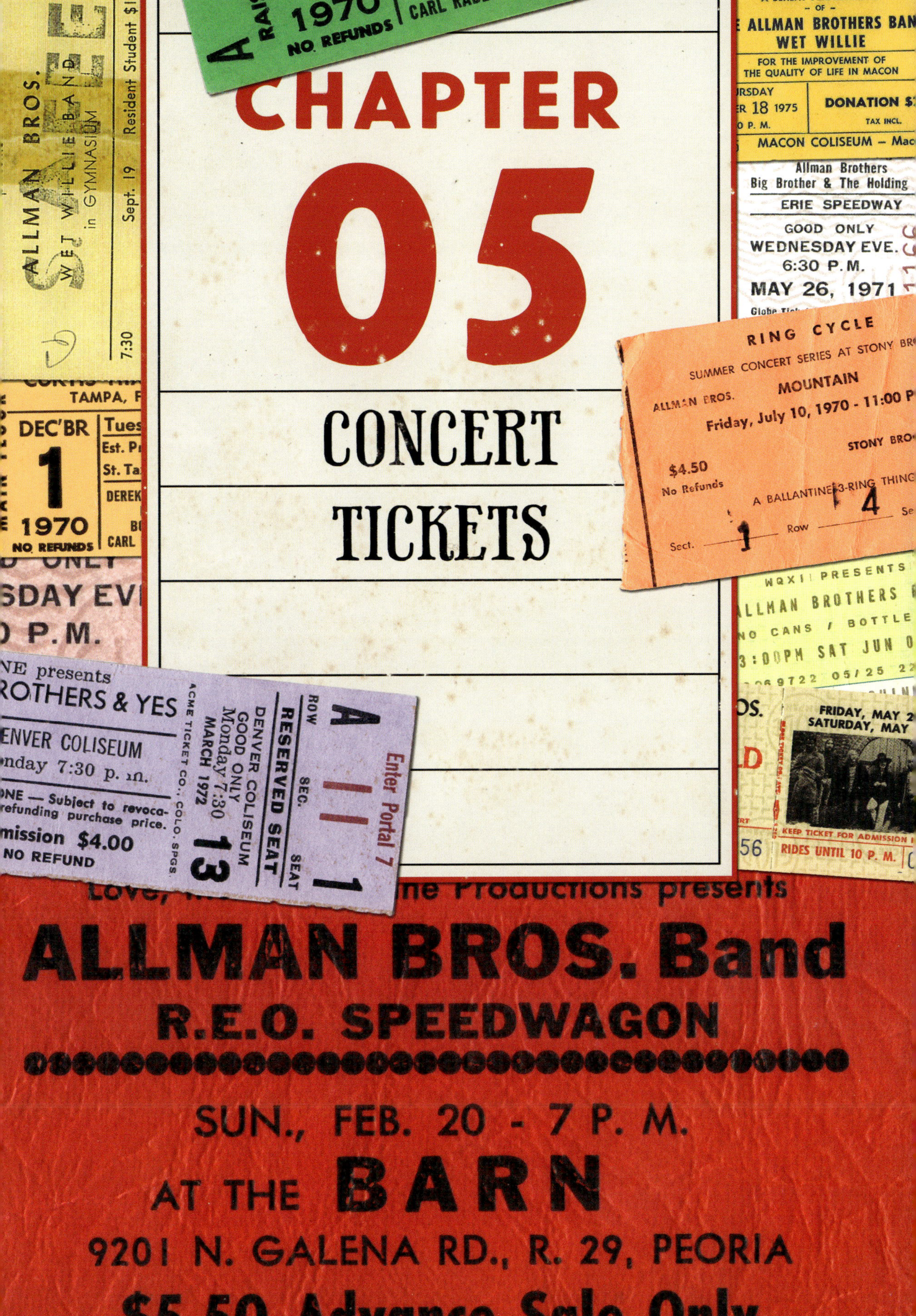
CHAPTER
05
CONCERT
TICKETS
1970
NO REFUNDS
ALLMAN BROS.
WET WILLIE BAND
in GYMNASIUM
Sept. 19
7:30
A BENEFIT PERFORMANCE
- OF -
ALLMAN BROTHERS
WET WILLIE
FOR THE IMPROVEMENT OF
THE QUALITY OF LIFE IN MACON
18 1975
DONATION
TAX INCL.
MACON COLISEUM
Allman Brothers
Big Brother & The Holding
ERIE SPEEDWAY
GOOD ONLY
WEDNESDAY EVE.
6:30 P.M.
MAY 26, 1971
TAMPA,
DEC'BR
1
1970
NO REFUNDS
RING CYCLE
SUMMER CONCERT SERIES AT STONY
ALLMAN BROS.
MOUNTAIN
Friday, July 10, 1970 - 11:00
$4.50
No Refunds
A BALLANTINE 3-RING THING
Sect. 1
Row 4
WQXI PRESENTS
NO CANS / BOTTLE
ROTHERS & YES
ENVER COLISEUM
Monday 7:30 p.m.
mission $4.00
NO REFUND
A
Enter Portal 7
RESERVED SEAT
DENVER COLISEUM
GOOD ONLY
Monday 7:30
MARCH 1972
13
ACME TICKET CO., COLO. SPGS.
FRIDAY, MAY
SATURDAY, MAY
KEEP TICKET FOR ADMISSION
RIDES UNTIL 10 P.M.
Productions presents
ALLMAN BROS. Band
R.E.O. SPEEDWAGON
SUN., FEB. 20 - 7 P. M.
AT THE BARN
9201 N. GALENA RD., R. 29, PEORIA
$5.50 Advance Sale Only

WILLIE PERKINS

Many early Allman Brothers Band concerts were held in nightclubs, music halls, and small venues and often required no ticket at all. Concertgoers simply paid the admission cost and walked in. There was no reserved seating. Later concerts in auditoriums, gymnasiums, arenas, and outdoor sports stadiums required a ticket for reserved, non-reserved, or festival seating. Festival seating did not offer a literal seat, just space for sitting or standing. This was often used for outdoor shows such as parks and sports stadiums.

The concert promoter provided printed tickets in a quantity that matched the seating capacity of the venue. Imprinted upon each ticket was the date, time, and place of the event plus the name of the artist, promoter, price, a seat number (if applicable), and a ticket number. If The Allman Brothers Band was to be paid a flat guaranteed amount for their performance no reconcilement of tickets sold was necessary unless there was evidence that excessive tickets had been printed which would materially change the gross proceeds. If they were working for a guaranteed amount plus a percentage of box office receipts, the box office receipts had to be verified by reconciling the number of tickets printed less unsold tickets, if any. A certain amount of complimentary tickets were allowed for authorized guests of the band and promoter. All of this was done the night of the concert, usually during the performance by the promoter and the band's tour manager. Of course, if a promoter had larceny in his heart he could secretly print additional tickets above and beyond the stated capacity of the venue often with a confederate from the venue. The band's tour manager was responsible for detecting and thwarting such conduct, but it was difficult to stop this practice completely.

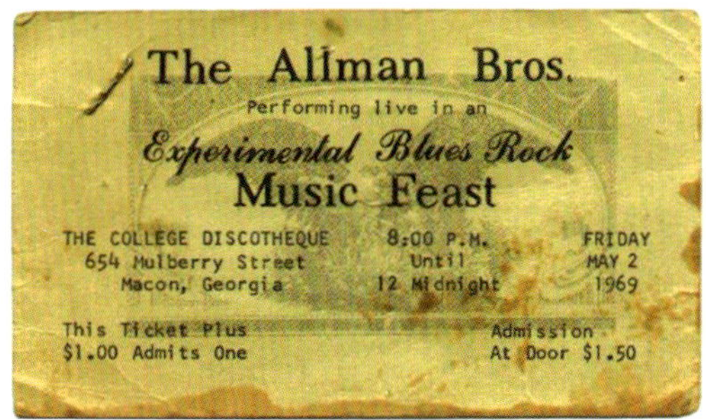

Band's first paid performance in Macon, *Kirk West collection.*

JACK WESTON

Vintage Allman Brothers Band concert tickets are highly coveted collectibles for many of their fans. Sometimes specific venues are the primary focus of a collection of tickets. Other times many different venues and time frames comprise a collection. Some collectors primarily collect tickets that correlate to the period that Duane Allman was still alive. Others will collect examples beyond this period and extend it to when Berry Oakley died nearly a year later in November of 1972. Untorn or unused tickets in mint condition from some of the Duane Allman era or better known shows are the most coveted and bring the highest prices in the collector market. One of my favorite Allman Brothers Band tickets was used for the "Pirates World" shows held on May 29-30, 1970, in Dania, Florida. This ticket has a photo of the band on the right hand side for the Saturday show. It was printed by Globe Ticket Company which can be seen in the watermark of the ticket.

Rare and valuable tickets should always be conserved and protected whenever possible. Mylar protection sleeves as well as acid free storage materials work best. If tickets are stored in a binder, Mylar page inserts or equivalent inert materials should be utilized. When tickets are framed behind glass for display, UV glass should be used to prevent fading of printing and paper over time.

Photo on ticket by Twiggs Lyndon, *Jack Weston collection.*

A

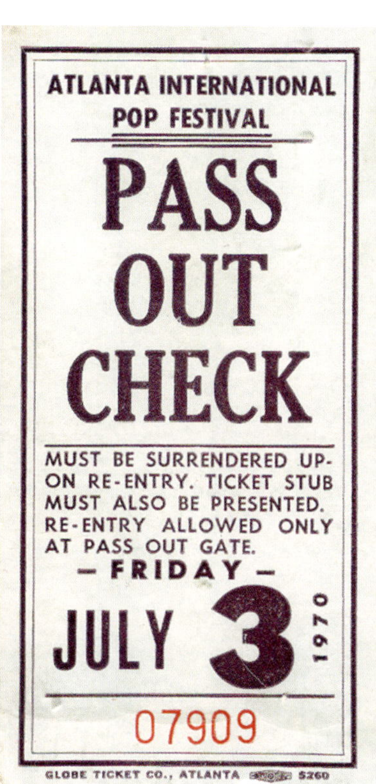

B

C

D

A Duane barely got there in time to perform. *Courtesy Mike Bagwell, Jack Weston collection.*

B Pass out check was for going in and out of concert venue. These were not used after this concert was declared open and free. *Courtesy Mike Bagwell, Jack Weston collection.*

C A favorite venue of the band. *Jack Weston collection.*

D A large regional festival held in a western town setting. *Jack Weston collection.*

ABOVE: The first of two shows that Duane Allman performed with Derek and The Dominos. *Courtesy Eric Clapton, Jack Weston collection;* **BELOW:** One of the band's first big financial paydays and headline arena shows.

ABOVE: Duane was personally and professionally close to Delaney and Bonnie Bramlett, *Jack Weston collection;* **MIDDLE:** Tampa, Florida; **BELOW:** S.U.N.Y. Stony Brook.

ABOVE: *Jack Weston collection;* **MIDDLE:** Allman name misspelled on ticket. *Jack Weston collection;* **BELOW:** Legendary outdoor concert that, at the time, was the largest concert attendance ever. *Courtesy The Allman Brothers Band Museum at The Big House.*

COMPLIMENTARY TICKET

DON KIRSHNER
in association with
PHIL WALDEN
present:
AN EVENING WITH
THE ALLMAN BROTHERS BAND
at the
GRAND OPERA HOUSE
MACON, GEORGIA
MONDAY, SEPT. 10, 1973
SHOW TIME: 7:30
DOORS OPEN: 6:45
must be seated by 7:30 p.m. for admission

NOT TO BE SOLD

ABOVE: Complimentary ticket for television show taped in Macon. *Jack Weston collection;* **MIDDLE:** Ticket for concert in New Jersey. *Jack Weston collection;* **BELOW:** Advance ticket for concert in Atlanta. *Jack Weston collection.*

ABOVE: Day of show ticket—largest concert event ever held at Atlanta stadium. *Kirk West collection;* **BELOW:** Proceeds from this concert were donated to various local charities. *Jack Weston collection.*

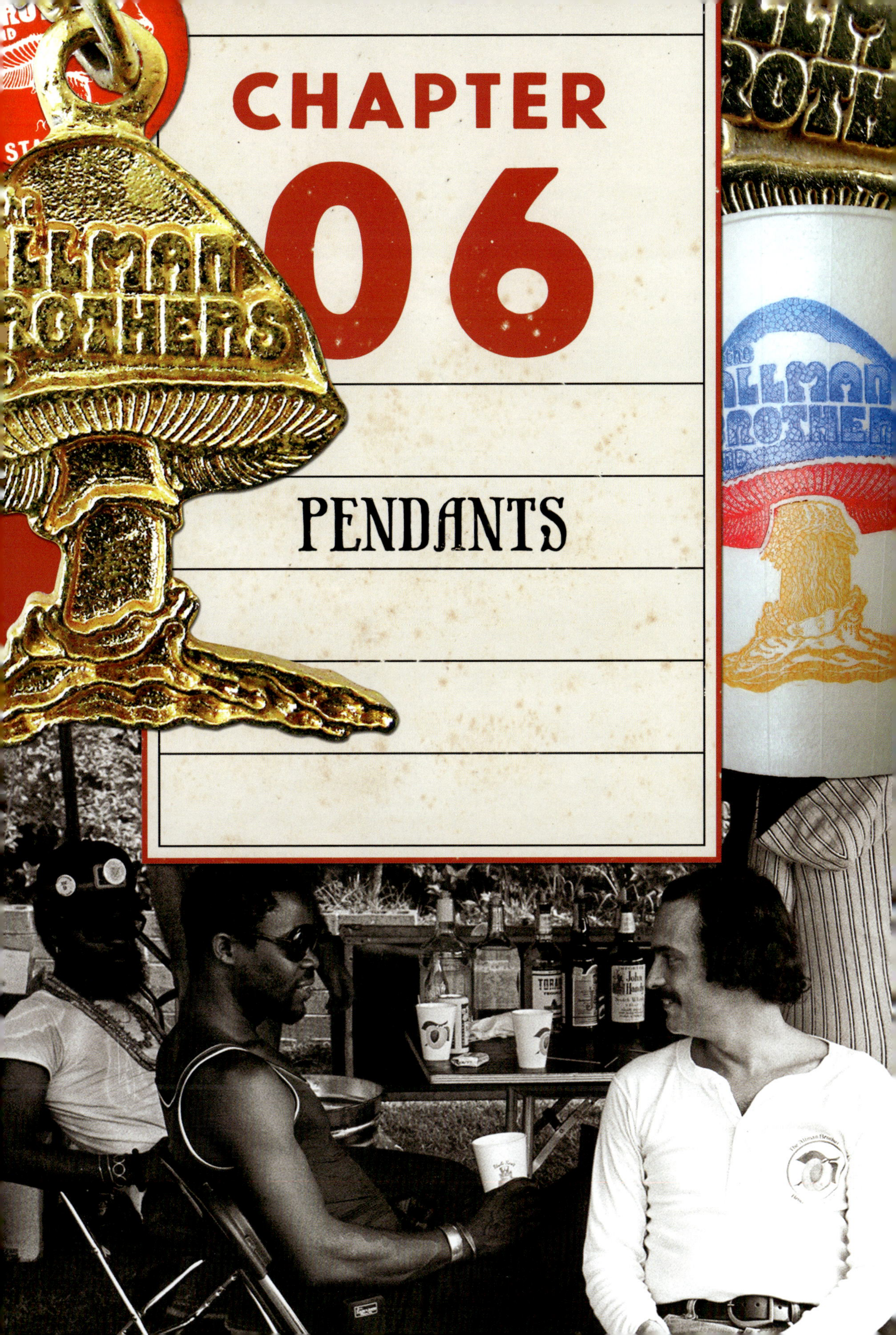

CHAPTER 06

PENDANTS

WILLIE PERKINS

My original mushroom pendant was unfortunately lost when I inadvertently left it hanging on a motel room doorknob in New Orleans. I purchased a replacement. Bill Snow also sold the band Styrofoam drinking cups imprinted with the mushroom logo which were used backstage at all band concerts and plastic mushroom embossed discs which were used as permanent employee all access passes. Later, the band's merchandising representatives at the time, The Great Southern Company, sold a nice souvenir gold colored metal mushroom pendant with chain which retailed for $5.00.

LEFT: Original 18K gold Allman Brothers Band mushroom pendant. *Jack Weston collection;* **RIGHT:** Great Southern Company imitation gold souvenir pendant, circa 1974, *Jack Weston collection.*

JACK WESTON

The first Allman Brothers Band pendants were produced in 1971. They were ordered by Phil Walden from his friend Bill Snow. Bill Snow was also the owner of a local funeral home, Memorial Chapel. He handled the funeral arrangements for Duane Allman. Mr. Snow contracted with a Macon jeweler who cast them in 18K gold. The classic mushroom image created by the Wonder Graphics team of James Flournoy Holmes and W. David Powell was used for the design of the pendant. There were various production runs and perhaps as many as 35 were produced overall. They were made for the original band members, road crew, close friends, family members, and Capricorn Records management. One of the first batches of pendants was received by Willie Perkins in December 1971. Producers Tom Dowd and Johnny Sandlin were among those who received one of these pendants. Tom Dowd wore his pendant practically every day for the rest of his life and Johnny Sandlin had his customized with a ruby insert.

LEFT: Original pendant cast for Duane Allman but never delivered due to his death. *Bill Snow collection, E. J. Devokaitis photo;* **RIGHT:** Original mushroom pendant with added ruby gemstone owned by Johnny Sandlin. *Anathalee G. Sandlin photo.*

CHAPTER 07

PROMOTIONAL ITEMS

WILLIE PERKINS

Most promotional items for The Allman Brothers Band from this period were produced and distributed by their record company, Capricorn Records. Two early and very rare items were a cigarette lighter embossed with the mushroom logo and cigarette rolling papers imprinted with the peach truck logo. A later item which is extremely rare is an automobile steering wheel "spinner" or "suicide knob." Most of these items were produced in relatively small quantities and primarily given to the band and crew, record company employees, and retail and wholesale record sales and distribution personnel. They were not available to the general public. There were also various posters and mobiles produced for in-store displays at retail record stores. These were called "pop" or "point of purchase" materials and most were eventually discarded. Capricorn Records and the band's various booking agencies also produced and distributed various 8 x 10 promotional photos.

The band itself used only a few promotional items, primarily pinback buttons and peel-off stickers. Some of these came from Capricorn Records and some were self-produced. There were various styles of each including the mushroom, peach truck, and brothers and sisters logos. Legendary band roadie, Red Dog, was known for tossing handfuls of pinback buttons into the crowd at concerts. Many of these items, though rare, are affordable collectibles. They are considered separately from similar items sold to the general public by the band's merchandisers.

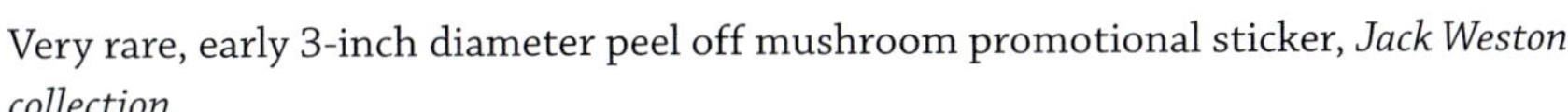

Very rare, early 3-inch diameter peel off mushroom promotional sticker, *Jack Weston collection.*

JACK WESTON

The Allman Brothers Band promotional items from the early 1970's are becoming more scarce as online auctions have depleted the number of remaining examples available for sale. They are still quite affordable though. The most sought after promotional items are stickers, pinbacks, and other items that are imprinted with the early classic The Allman Brothers Band mushroom logo.

The mushroom pinback button was approximately 1.625 inches in diameter with a black imprint on a white background and was produced by two firms. One version was made by N. G. Slater Corporation of New York City, their name printed on the rim of the pinback. The pin on this version stuck out approximately .25 inch on the back. The other company that produced this pinback did not print its name on it and the pin on the back is recessed with a clip.

Perhaps the most rare promotional stickers were the classic set of two mushroom stickers that came with "The Allman Brothers Band at Fillmore East" press kits. I have seen a couple of examples of these stickers. They are small and of slightly different sizes with the same imprint that the classic mushroom pinbacks had.

One of the rarest promotional items of the early 1970's is a nickel plated cigarette lighter with the classic mushroom logo. While most of these were given to the band, road crew, and extended family, some were in fact used for promotional purposes and were given to concert promoters as well as record industry executives. According to Chank Middleton, longtime friend of Gregg Allman, one of these lighters was put in Duane Allman's shirt pocket before he was buried.

In 1974 a 3-inch pinback button was made to promote the European Tour. The design of this pinback has General Robert E. Lee on horseback with a confederate flag in the background. On the perimeter of this pinback is printed "The Allman Brothers Band European Campaign." This pinback is becoming more rare, however, high-grade examples can occasionally be obtained online and from other sources.

In 1969 The Allman Brothers Band had Dexter Press, Inc. of West Nyack, New York, make a postcard made to promote their first LP distributed by Atco Records. The front has a photo of the band in a creek at Otis Redding's farm. This image came from a photograph by

Stephen Paley. Stephen took many of the photos used for the band's early publicity images. Rosehill Cemetery in Macon, Georgia, was used extensively by Mr. Paley for many of the backdrops of these iconic publicity photos. Jim Marshall also took some of the photo images for publicity photos used to promote "The Allman Brothers Band Live At Fillmore East" LP.

Postcards were also produced by the band to promote their "Brothers and Sisters" LP in 1973. Capricorn Records produced a postcard to promote the "Saturday Night In Macon" TV show at the Grand Opera House in Macon, Georgia, on September 10, 1973.

Conservation methods should always be employed to protect promotional memorabilia. I use Mylar sleeves that have multiple pockets to protect pinbacks, postcards, stickers and other promotional items stored in binders.

Very early band promotional photo. *Jack Weston collection, Twiggs Lyndon photo.*

Early mushroom 8 x 10 peel off promotional sticker. *Jack Weston collection.*

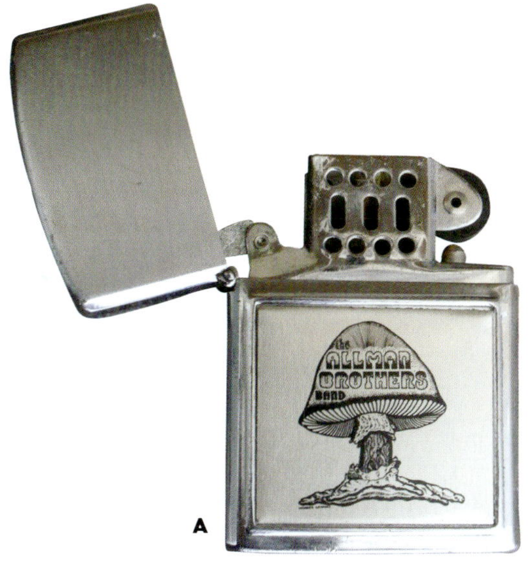

A

B

C

A Rare, early promotional lighter. Capricorn Records produced these for their staff, band, crew, VIPs, and customers. *Jack Weston collection.*

B 1.75-inch pinback promotional button. *Jack Weston collection.*

C 4 x 6, "Peach Truck" peel-off promotional sticker. *Jack Weston collection.*

ABOVE: Back and front view of "Eat A Peach" cigarette rolling papers. These were given away by Capricorn Records as a promotional item. *Jack Weston collection;* **BELOW:** "Peach Truck" sew-on patch. *Jack Weston collection.*

A “Eat A Peach” design cigarette lighter. *Jack Weston collection.*

B “Eat A Peach” 2.25-inch pinback button. *Jack Weston collection.*

C Rare, “Peach Truck” pin made in England. *Jack Weston collection.*

ABOVE: "Peach Truck" pin. *Jack Weston collection;* **BELOW:** "Brothers and Sisters" peel-off promotional sticker. *Jack Weston collection.*

ABOVE: Jumbo promotional postcard of band and crew at band's farm, 1972. *Jack Weston collection, Bill Meriwether photo;* **BELOW:** Rare promotional sticker for Capricorn Records in Europe. *Jack Weston collection.*

ABOVE: Front view promotional postcard for October 1973 TV show. *Jack Weston collection;* **BELOW:** 3-inch promotional pinback button for 1974 European tour. *Jack Weston collection.*

CHAPTER 08

VINTAGE PHOTOS

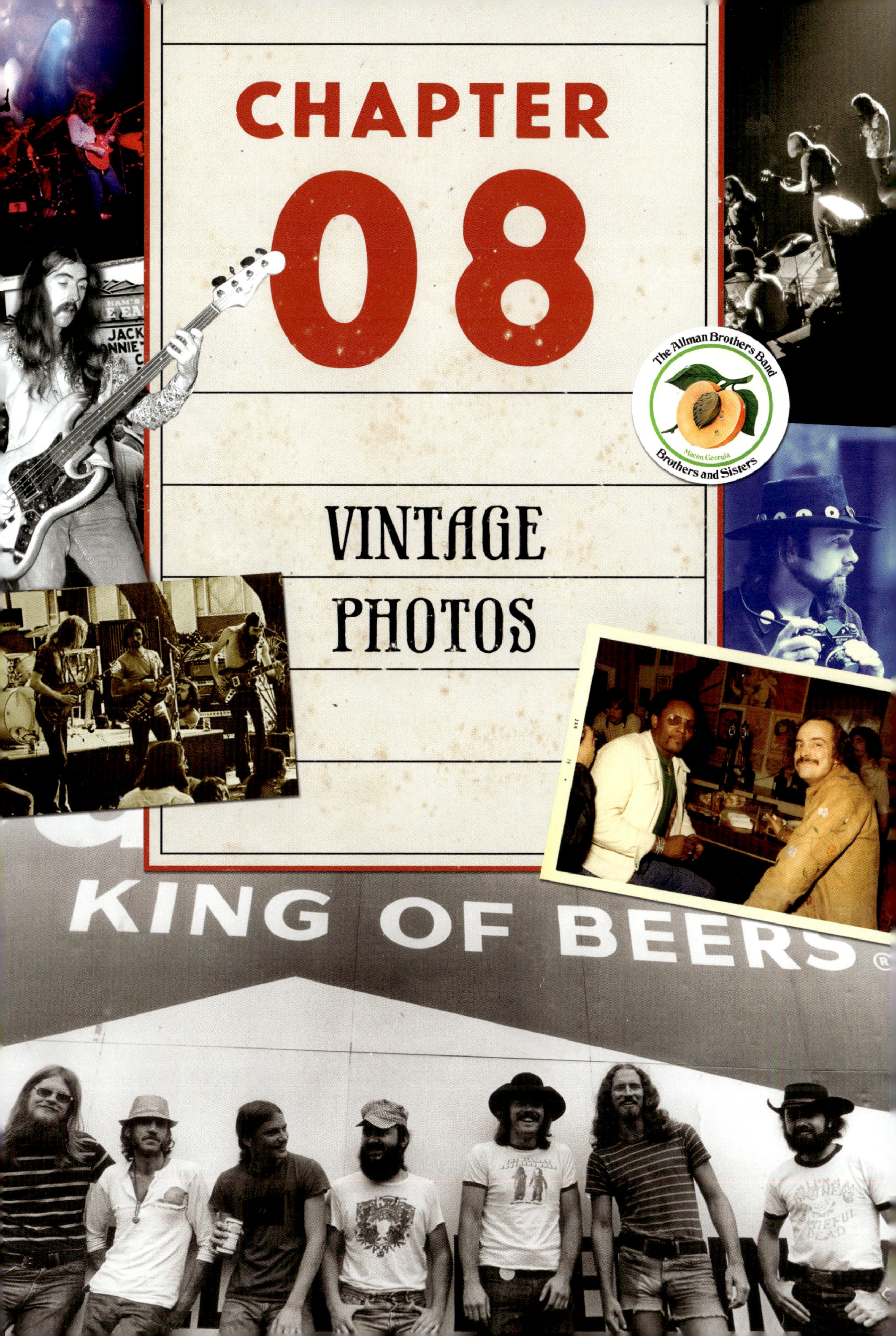

OPPOSITE: Rare, original 8 x 10 print of early time-lapse photo taken by Twiggs Lyndon in 1969. *Jack Weston collection, Twiggs Lyndon photo.*

WILLIE PERKINS

There is a large universe of photographs of The Allman Brothers Band from the early years. This is somewhat amazing because both Duane Allman and Berry Oakley passed away within three years of the band's formation.

Twiggs Lyndon, the band's first tour manager, was a good amateur photographer and he took many early shots of them both in Macon and on the road. Of particular interest is a series of photos he took of the band at the Grand Canyon on their first tour west. There are also some interesting family snapshots taken in and around the band's communal residence in Macon known as The Big House. These shots, especially some of the Oakley family, show a completely different facet of the band's existence and some are quite touching.

Early on, professional photographers were engaged, usually by Capricorn Records, for the purpose of taking publicity stills and album artwork. Stephen Paley and Jim Marshall are the two best known of these. Sidney Smith of New Orleans more or less had carte blanche to photograph the band in both professional and personal surroundings during the early and mid-1970's. Many other well known professional photographers also shot the band for magazine articles and on speculation. These photos consist of posed, candid, and performance shots.

I am constantly amazed by the number of band photos which turn up on fan websites and social media sites, like Facebook, on a daily basis.

While quality prints from well known photographers can cost upwards of a thousand dollars or more each there are literally hundreds of photos which are downloadable from the internet for no cost at all.

JACK WESTON

Photographs need to be protected and conserved with the appropriate conservation methods. I use Mylar protective sleeves and sheets to protect all the photographs in my collection. Type D Mylar offers the best conservation protection and is considered by many curators to be museum grade. I have repaired minor corner tears in photographs using Lineco Neutral pH adhesive with excellent results. Another product I have used extensively for cleaning photos is Pec-12 which is made by Photographic Solutions, Inc. This product is an excellent archival photographic emulsion cleaner. One case in point occurred about fifteen years ago when I acquired a large, rare 14 x 20 photograph of Duane Allman which was likely printed in the 1970's. This photograph was taken by Jon Levicke at the Whiskey A-Go-Go in Los Angeles on October 2, 1971. It was dry mounted by Mr. Levicke on poster board with his signature on the board just below the print. An amazing image, but unfortunately someone along the way had pretty much compromised the emulsion by trying to hide various original negative imperfections using a black magic marker pen. Also, the entire emulsion had been sprayed with a thick lacquer in uneven strokes. I initially used a professional photograph emulsion cleaning pad along with Pec-12 in a couple of inconspicuous areas to test it and to my amazement it was working perfectly. I then proceeded to clean the entire emulsion successfully removing all the lacquer overspray. Also the majority of nearly thirty black marker marks were successfully removed using this method. It took me approximately four hours to complete but was well worth the effort. The end result was gratifying considering that this print initially appeared to be a hopeless cause. If in doubt always consult with and consider hiring a professional photograph conservator to repair and restore valuable photographs. Graphics programs such as Adobe Photoshop® and others can be employed to correct and restore image damage with excellent results.

ABOVE: Duane Allman in 1969. *Twiggs Lyndon photo;* **BELOW:** The band at the Grand Canyon on their first trip to the west coast. *Twiggs Lyndon photo.*

ABOVE: Butch Trucks at the Grand Canyon enjoying the view. *Twiggs Lyndon photo;*
BELOW: The band on the porch at "Idlewild South" house. *Twiggs Lyndon photo.*

ABOVE: The band at the first LP cover site on College Street in Macon, Georgia. *Twiggs Lyndon photo;* **BELOW:** Twiggs Lyndon photographing the band onstage.

ABOVE: Very early photo of Jaimoe (location unknown). *Twiggs Lyndon photo;* **BELOW:** Duane Allman outdoors. *Twiggs Lyndon photo*; **OPPOSITE:** Duane Allman at Willingham Chapel, Mercer University in Macon, Georgia. *"Crazy" Jim Wiggins photo, All rights reserved.*

ABOVE: Twiggs Lyndon preparing to take a photo. **BELOW:** Duane Allman onstage hittin' the note. *Twiggs Lyndon photo.*

ABOVE: Duane Allman playing slide on his 1961 Gibson Les Paul (SG) Standard bought from Dickey Betts. *Twiggs Lyndon photo;* **BELOW:** Berry Oakley.

ABOVE: Duane Allman with Eric Clapton onstage at Derek and The Dominos concert in Tampa, Florida, December 1, 1970. *Courtesy Eric Clapton, Allman Family Archives;* **MIDDLE:** Duane Allman onstage at Macon Coliseum, 1971. *W. Robert Johnson photo;* **BELOW:** *(left to right)* Duane Allman, Dickey Betts, and Berry Oakley onstage at Macon Coliseum, 1971. *W. Robert Johnson photo;* **OPPOSITE:** Band onstage at Macon Coliseum, 1971. *W. Robert Johnson photo.*

PREVIOUS: The Allman Brothers Band with Joe's Lights at Fillmore East, June 27, 1971. ©*Amalie R. Rothschild;* **ABOVE:** Gregg and Duane on stage at Fillmore East, June 27, 1971. © *Amalie R. Rothschild.*

ABOVE: Duane Allman and Dickey Betts at Fillmore East, June 27, 1971. © *Amalie R. Rothschild;* **BELOW:** Fans outside Fillmore East, January 1970. © *Amalie R. Rothschild.*

ABOVE: Berry Oakley and Duane Allman on the balcony at the Atlanta Municipal Auditorium, July 17, 1971. *Carter Tomassi photo;* **BELOW:** Berry Oakley, Brittany, and Linda Oakley in front of The Big House. *Billy Ratliff photo;* **OPPOSITE:** Duane Allman at Fillmore East, June 27, 1971. © *Amalie R. Rothschild.*

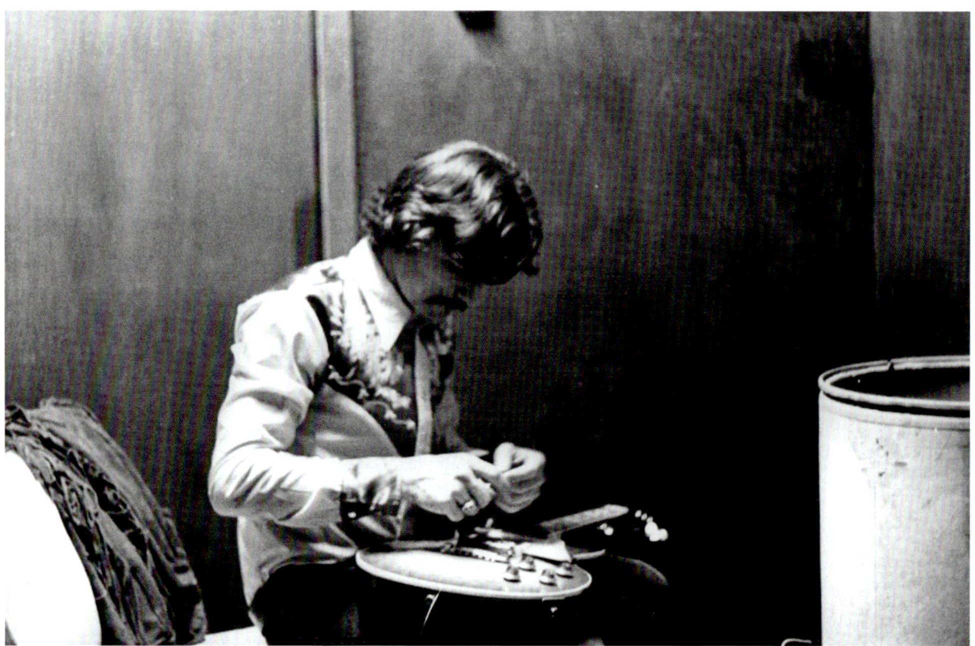

ABOVE: Behind the band at The Warehouse, New Orleans, December 31, 1972. *Sidney Smith photo/SidneySmithPhotos.com;* **BELOW:** Dickey Betts backstage at The Warehouse, New Orleans, December 31, 1971. *Jack Weston collection.*

Berry Oakley at The Warehouse, New Orleans. *Sidney Smith photo/SidneySmithPhotos.com.*

Sandy Bluesky Wabegijig in Indian headdress. *Twiggs Lyndon photo.*

ABOVE: Roadcrew member Buffalo Evans. *Kirk West collection;* **BELOW:** Tour manager Willie Perkins with briefcase waiting for the band. *Kirk West collection.*

Lamar Williams and Chuck Leavell at band farm. *Herb Kossover photo.*

ABOVE: Janice Blair Allman and Gregg Allman at Betts/Bluesky wedding. *Sidney Smith photo/SidneySmithPhotos.com;* **BELOW:** Sandy Bluesky Wabegijig and Dickey Betts cutting cake at their wedding. *Sidney Smith photo/SidneySmithPhotos.com.*

ABOVE: Gregg Allman onstage playing Gibson Les Paul (SG) guitar. **BELOW:** Earl "Speedo" Simms and Willie Perkins at one of many bars. *Kirk West collection.*

ABOVE: *(left to right)* Lamar Williams, Jaimoe, and Willie Perkins at Capricorn Records barbecue. *Sidney Smith photo/SidneySmithPhotos.com;* **BELOW:** *(left to right)* Stage crew: John Gilly, Red Dog, Mike Artz, Andy Lyndon, Buddy Thornton, Larry Brantley, and Twiggs Lyndon, Atlanta Stadium, June 1, 1974. *Jack Weston collection, used with permission of Anheuser-Busch, LLC. All rights reserved.*

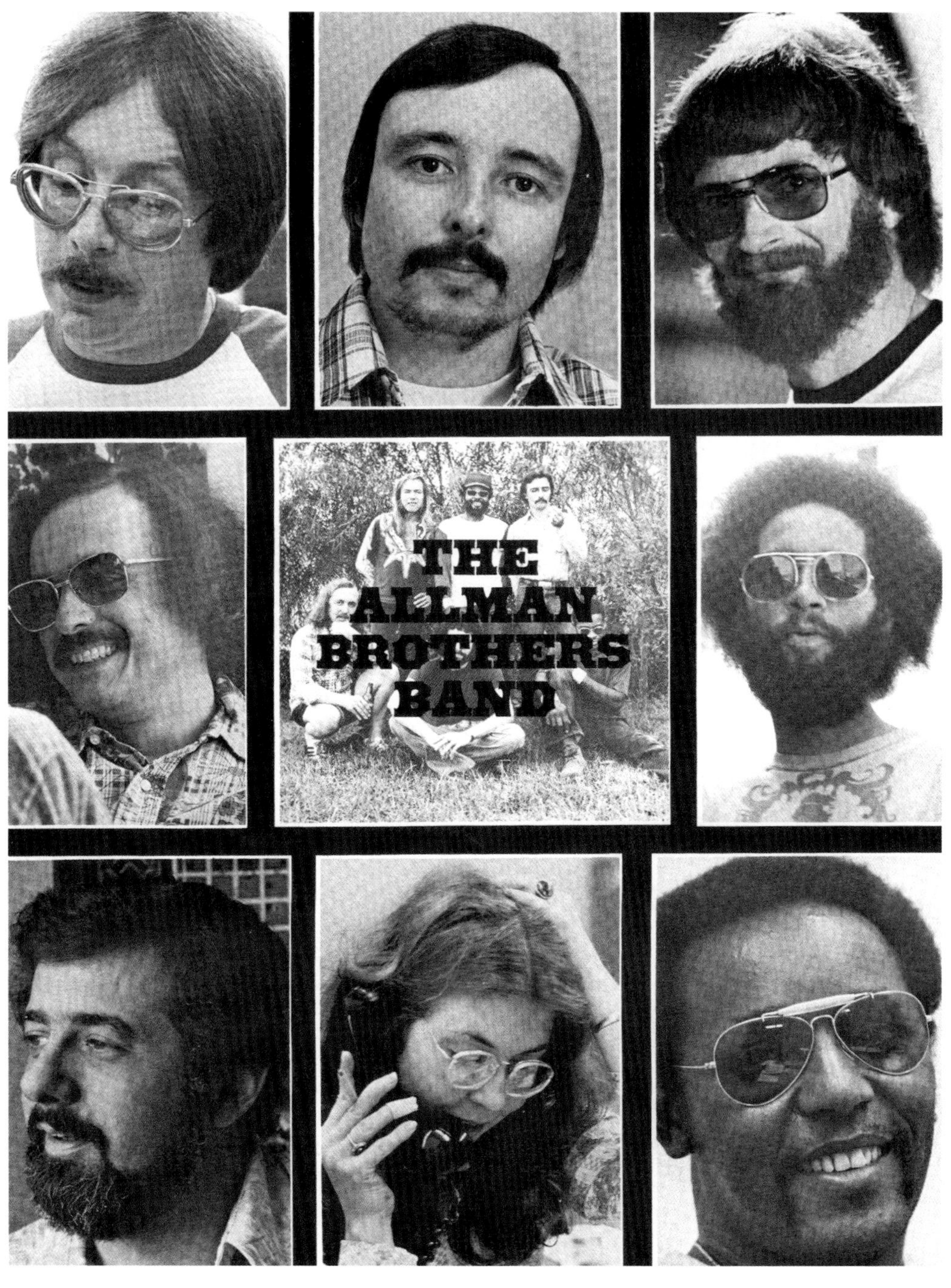

Management team: *(clockwise from top left)* Scott Hayes, Charles Bignon, "Scooter" Herring, "Chank" Middleton, "Speedo" Simms, Jana Vickers, "Bunky" Odom, and Willie Perkins. © *Gilbert Lee photo/gilbertlee.com.*

ABOVE: The Big House, circa 1974. *Courtesy The Allman Brothers Band Museum at The Big House;* **NEXT PAGE:** Memorabilia display at The Big House Museum. *Courtesy The Allman Brothers Band Museum at The Big House, E. J. Devokaitis photo.*

Great
Speckled
The BIRd
PREMIER TALENT ASSOCIATES, INC.
EARTBREAKERS
Marshall

Fender JAZZ BASS
ALLMAN BROTHERS
Fender
Fender

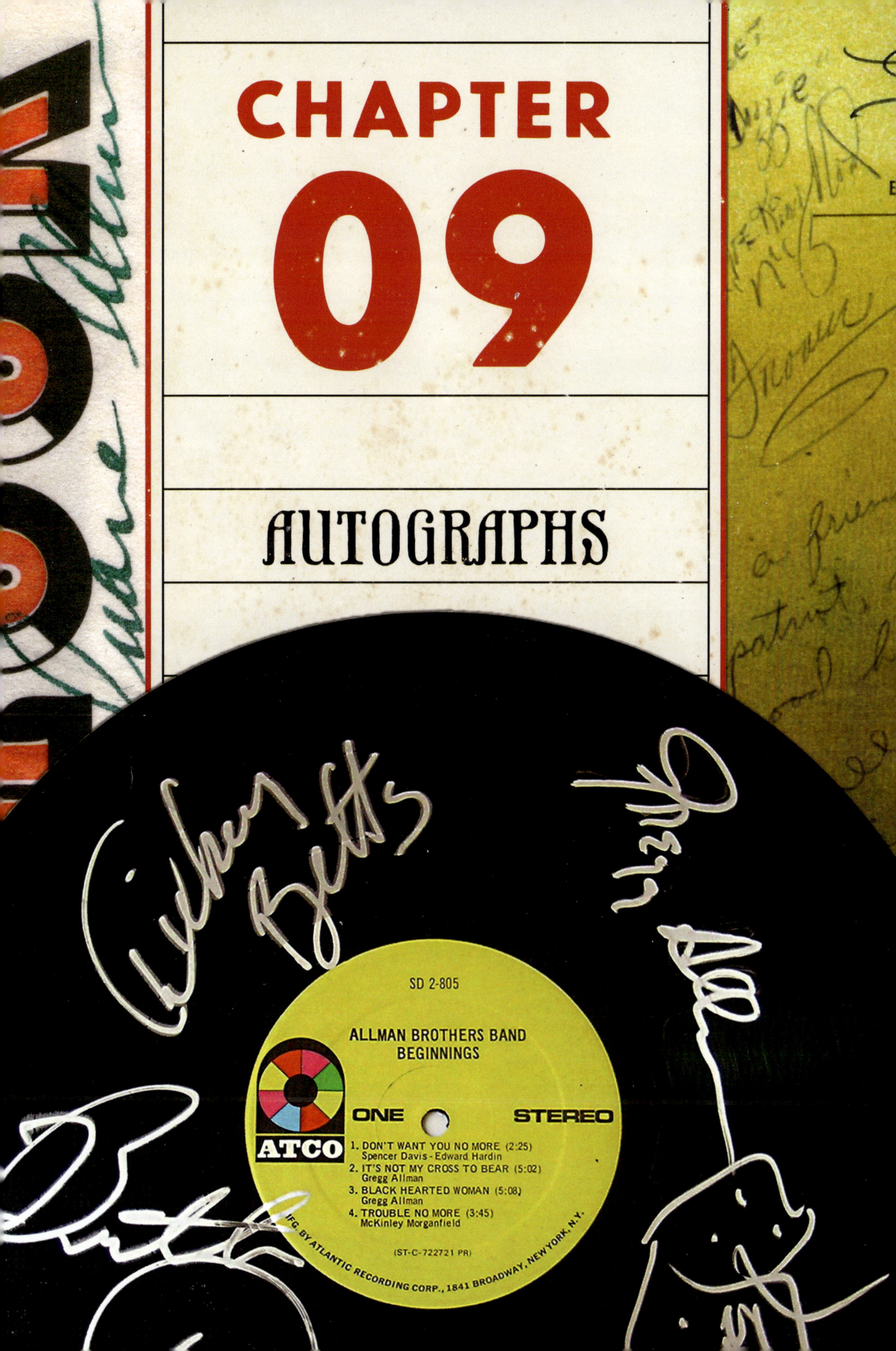
CHAPTER
09
AUTOGRAPHS
SD 2-805
ALLMAN BROTHERS BAND
BEGINNINGS
ATCO
ONE
STEREO
1. DON'T WANT YOU NO MORE (2:25)
Spencer Davis - Edward Hardin
2. IT'S NOT MY CROSS TO BEAR (5:02)
Gregg Allman
3. BLACK HEARTED WOMAN (5:08)
Gregg Allman
4. TROUBLE NO MORE (3:45)
McKinley Morganfield
(ST-C-722721 PR)
MFG. BY ATLANTIC RECORDING CORP., 1841 BROADWAY, NEW YORK, N.Y.

WILLIE PERKINS

The term fan comes from the word fanatic and fans of The Allman Brothers Band were indeed enthusiastic about their favorite musical group. The entire group including myself and other crew members were often besieged for our signatures. We all signed various items including album covers, photos, autograph books, scraps of paper, menus and napkins in bars and restaurants and even the occasional human torso. Of course, Duane Allman was the most popular of the group and because of his early passing before he and the band had attained huge popularity, his autograph is the most sought after today.

Band members in the early days also signed business checks and although these are not technically autographs they are very rare and highly collectible. Duane Allman's name also appears as the signatory on many concert personal appearance contracts, however virtually all of these were signed by booking agent employees under a limited power of attorney. The band members were rarely in proximity of the booking agency when contracts were prepared. Some of these contracts with affixed signatures have been sold as genuine by well meaning but misinformed individuals. Also, there are some blatant forgeries of band members' signatures by unscrupulous individuals. Sometimes office personnel signed fan requests for autographs as a matter of convenience. These are known as secretarial signatures. As with any collectible the term caveat emptor applies. Let the buyer beware and never pay high prices for any autographs without having them authenticated.

Original Duane Allman signature. *Jack Weston collection.*

JACK WESTON

The majority of Allman Brothers Band autographs I have seen from the classic era that this book covers (1969–1976) were written with ball point and felt tipped pens. I have also seen a few authentic examples signed in fountain pen. Lyrics written by Gregg Allman or Dickey Betts, while technically not autographs are extremely rare and command the highest prices. Also letters written by any of the founding members during this classic time frame are considered highly collectible. If acquiring a rare Allman Brothers Band autograph make sure to compare it with known authentic examples. Forensic examination by a certified handwriting professional may be needed for valuable investment grade pieces. Whenever in doubt always purchase autographs from reputable dealers that provide a money back guarantee. If displaying autographs in a frame always use UV glass to prevent the ink from fading over time. As with other Allman Brothers Band collectibles using Mylar sleeves is an excellent way to protect your valuable investment.

ABOVE: Copy of first LP owned by Red Dog and signed by original band members. *Stephen Paley photo;* **OPPOSITE:** "Beginnings" LP signed by four founding band members. *Jack Weston collection.*

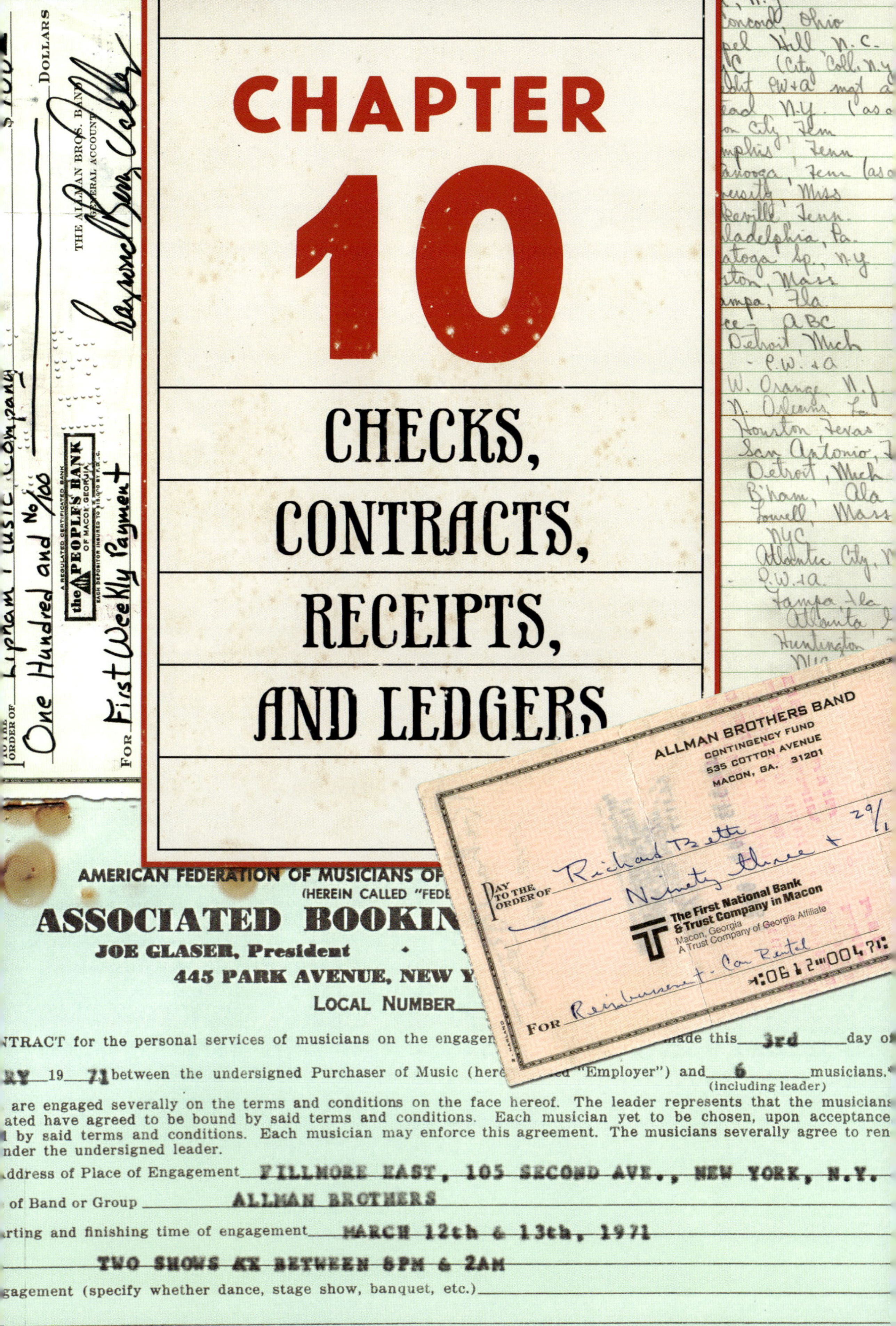

CHAPTER
10
CHECKS, CONTRACTS, RECEIPTS, AND LEDGERS
ALLMAN BROTHERS BAND
CONTINGENCY FUND
535 COTTON AVENUE
MACON, GA. 31201
PAY TO THE ORDER OF
FOR
The First National Bank & Trust Company in Macon
Macon, Georgia
A Trust Company of Georgia Affiliate
AMERICAN FEDERATION OF MUSICIANS OF
(HEREIN CALLED "FEDE
ASSOCIATED BOOKIN
JOE GLASER, President
445 PARK AVENUE, NEW Y
LOCAL NUMBER
FILLMORE EAST, 105 SECOND AVE., NEW YORK, N.Y.
ALLMAN BROTHERS
MARCH 12th & 13th, 1971
TWO SHOWS BETWEEN 8PM & 2AM

WILLIE PERKINS

Even creative and artistic endeavors such as a band require some method of recording business transactions and retaining records of them. Twiggs Lyndon set up such a system for The Allman Brothers Band based on his prior experience as a tour manager for other artists. When I was hired in June 1970 after Twiggs' incarceration I was handed a box of receipts, a checkbook, and a few dollars and coins in petty cash by drummer Butch Trucks along with the cheerful challenge of "Good Luck!"

I did not have an accounting degree but had taken some accounting courses in high school and college. That, combined with my experience as a commercial bank auditor enabled me to set up a rudimentary double entry bookkeeping system based on debits and credits manually posted to various journals and ledgers. An outside certified public accountant was retained to verify my bookkeeping and to prepare income tax returns for the band and the individual members. We were fortunate never to be audited or have any tax returns challenged by the IRS. Much of the band's history can be followed simply by reviewing petty cash receipts, cancelled checks and ledgers showing income and expenses. As such, these documents are desirable collectibles.

Twiggs Lyndon had originally opened a commercial checking account known as the general account. Only a band member could sign a check, but Twiggs kept the checkbook, prepared checks as necessary and then garnered a band member signature. This system was retained when I was hired, but after a few months the band suggested I be added as a signer negating having to find a band member to sign every check issued. As the band's business structure and needs changed over time from partnerships to a corporation, additional checking accounts were opened. These included a payroll account, farm account for their property in Juliette, Georgia, and pension and profit-sharing accounts. Many of these checks are interesting from a historical perspective because of the transactions they show. All of the early checks signed by band members are collectible but those signed by Duane Allman are the most valuable.

Many collectors enjoy owning Allman Brothers Band personal appearance contracts especially those from historically noteworthy concerts. As noted earlier virtually all of these contain only a facsimile signature of a band member, but are still highly collectible. Be advised, these were multi-copied forms in multiple colors. The artist and purchaser copies are the most collectible with the union and office copies of much lesser value. The rarest of all contracts are the personal management, recording, and music writer-publisher contracts between the band members and those various entities. The signatures on these are all almost positively legitimate because of the nature of the agreements. The usual collector cautions apply with only original items and not with copies, facsimiles, or forgeries having any real value.

THE ALLMAN BROS. BAND
GENERAL ACCOUNT
5001
64-1137
612
DATE February 1, 1970
PAY TO THE ORDER OF Lipham Music Company $100.00
One Hundred and No/100 DOLLARS
the PEOPLES BANK OF MACON, GEORGIA
THE ALLMAN BROS. BAND
GENERAL ACCOUNT
FOR First Weekly Payment

THE ALLMAN BROS. BAND
GENERAL ACCOUNT
5012
64-1137
612
DATE March 30, 1970
PAY TO THE ORDER OF Duane Allman $175.00
One Hundred Seventy Five and 00/100 DOLLARS
the PEOPLES BANK OF MACON, GEORGIA
THE ALLMAN BROS. BAND
GENERAL ACCOUNT
FOR Rent on New House

ABOVE: First weekly payment on band line of credit at Lipham Music Company for equipment purchased in 1969. *Jack Weston collection;* **BELOW:** Monthly rental payment on The Big House.

JACK WESTON

The first Allman Brothers Band general account check drafted (#5001) was for the first weekly payment for guitars, amplifiers and other gear that the band purchased from Lipham Music Company of Gainesville, Florida, in early 1969. This check was signed by Berry Oakley as Raymond Berry Oakley on February 1, 1970. Buster Lipham, who made this sale, advanced the band equipment interest free for almost a year until this check was written as the first weekly payment. Today the most desirable Allman Brothers Band checks to collect are these Lipham Music Company checks signed by Duane Allman. Based on the early checks I have seen, Berry Oakley signed the majority of all the general account checks.

Very few of the Allman Brothers Band performance contracts were signed by band members. I have seen just two that I am confidant were actually signed by Duane Allman. Most of the other contracts I have seen are signed by booking agency personnel who had power of attorney to sign as Duane Allman or Gregg Allman. A few contracts that I have seen were signed by Berry Oakley and those have his authentic signature.

Most of the ledgers and receipts are in the permanent archives of The Big House Museum in Macon, Georgia. Some are also held in private collections. These documents hold invaluable historical data for current and future research.

Again, as with all paper ephemera, conservation is necessary to protect and preserve these artifacts for future generations. I obtain my Mylar sleeves from coin and stamp dealers that sell them for the protection of various denominations of currency. There are different sizes available so that obtaining the correct size for checks or documents is easy to accomplish.

THE ALLMAN BROS. BAND
PAYROLL ACCOUNT

1001

64-1137
612

DATE January 26, 1970

PAY TO THE ORDER OF Howard Duane Allman $ 61 40/100

Sixty One and 40/100 DOLLARS

A REGULATED CERTIFICATED BANK
the PEOPLES BANK OF MACON, GEORGIA
EACH DEPOSITOR INSURED TO $15,000 BY F.D.I.C.

THE ALLMAN BROS. BAND
PAYROLL ACCOUNT

Gregory L. Allman

⑆0612⑉1137⑆ 0 11 246 1⑈

14- HARLAND

THE ALLMAN BROS. BAND
GENERAL ACCOUNT

FEB 16 1970

5002

N.P.
FEB 11 1970
COLLECTION
64-45

64-1137
612

DATE February 1, 1970

PAY TO THE ORDER OF The Citizens and Southern National Bank $ 281 10/100

Two Hundred Eighty One and 10/100 DOLLARS

A REGULATED CERTIFICATED BANK
the PEOPLES BANK OF MACON, GEORGIA
EACH DEPOSITOR INSURED TO $15,000 BY F.D.I.C.

FEB 6 1970
L. CHERRY
64-45

THE ALLMAN BROS. BAND
GENERAL ACCOUNT

FOR First Winnebago Payment

Johnny L. Johnson

⑆0612⑉1137⑆ 0 11 248 8⑈ ⑆0000028110⑆

2- HARLAND

ABOVE: Early payroll account check signed by Gregg Allman and endorsed by Duane Allman as Howard Duane Allman. *Courtesy The Allman Brothers Band Museum at The Big House*; **BELOW:** First payment on Winnebago camper used for touring signed by Jaimoe. *Jack Weston collection.*

THE ALLMAN BROS. BAND
GENERAL ACCOUNT

5010

64-1137
612

DATE March 22, 1970

PAY TO THE ORDER OF Lipham Music Company $200.00

Two Hundred and 00/100 DOLLARS

A REGULATED CERTIFICATED BANK
the PEOPLES BANK
OF MACON, GEORGIA
EACH DEPOSITOR INSURED TO $15,000 BY F.D.I.C.

FOR Eighth Weekly Payment

THE ALLMAN BROS. BAND
GENERAL ACCOUNT

Duane Allman

⑆0612⑈1137⑆ 0 11 248 8⑈ ⑈0000020000⑈

2- HARLAND

THE ALLMAN BROS. BAND
GENERAL ACCOUNT

5040

64-1137
612

DATE May 5 1970

PAY TO THE ORDER OF Lipham Music Co. $200.00

Two Hundred and 00/100 DOLLARS

PAID
PEOPLES BANK of MACON
MAY 18 1970
MACON, GEORGIA

A REGULATED CERTIFICATED BANK
the PEOPLES BANK
OF MACON, GEORGIA
EACH DEPOSITOR INSURED TO $15,000 BY F.D.I.C.

FOR 13th weekly Payment

THE ALLMAN BROS. BAND
GENERAL ACCOUNT

Claude Trucks

⑆0612⑈1137⑆ 0 11 248 8⑈ ⑈0000020000⑈

2- HARLAND

THE ALLMAN BROS. BAND
GENERAL ACCOUNT

5085

64-1137
612

DATE 6/8 1970

PAY TO THE ORDER OF Gregg Allman $20.00

Twenty and no/100 DOLLARS

PAID
PEOPLES BANK
9 1970
MACON, GEORGIA

A REGULATED CERTIFICATED BANK
the PEOPLES BANK
OF MACON, GEORGIA
EACH DEPOSITOR INSURED TO $15,000 BY F.D.I.C.

FOR salary advance

THE ALLMAN BROS. BAND
GENERAL ACCOUNT

Gregg L. Allman

⑆0612⑈1137⑆ 0 11 248 8⑈ ⑈0000002000⑈

2- HARLAND

ABOVE: Payments on a Lipham Music Company line of credit signed by Duane Allman (above) and Butch Trucks (below). *Jack Weston collection*; **BELOW:** Salary advance to Gregg Allman. The check was made out by Willie Perkins and signed by Gregg Allman. *Jack Weston collection.*

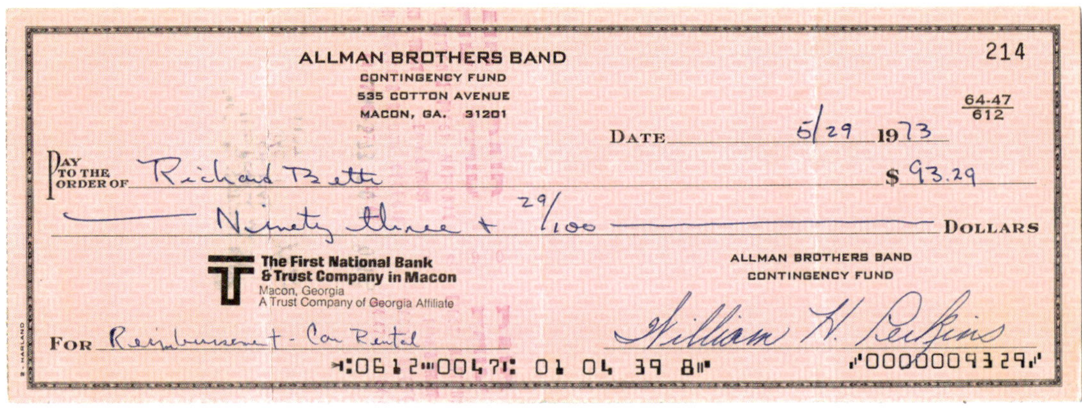

ALLMAN BROTHERS BAND
CONTINGENCY FUND
535 COTTON AVENUE
MACON, GA. 31201

214

64-47
612

DATE 5/29 1973

PAY TO THE ORDER OF Richard Betts $ 93.29

Ninety three + 29/100 DOLLARS

The First National Bank & Trust Company in Macon
Macon, Georgia
A Trust Company of Georgia Affiliate

ALLMAN BROTHERS BAND
CONTINGENCY FUND

FOR Reimbursement - Car Rental

William H. Perkins

⑆0612⑈0047⑆ 01 04 39 8⑈ ⑈0000009329⑈

BROTHERS PROPERTIES, INC. D/B/A
THE ALLMAN BROTHERS BAND
OPERATING ACCOUNT

469

64-249
611

12-15- 1975

PAY TO THE ORDER OF Twiggs M. Lyndon Jr. $ 390.86

THE SUM 390 DOLLS 86 CTS DOLLARS

MACON BANK & TRUST COMPANY
MACON, GEORGIA

THE ALLMAN BROTHERS BAND
OPERATING ACCOUNT

FOR net pay 12/14; Travel Pay thru 12/14/75

Charles N. Bignon

⑆0611⑈0249⑆ 006 318⑈ ⑈0000039086⑈

THE ALLMAN BROS. BAND
GENERAL ACCOUNT

5530

64-1137
612

DATE 6/17 1971

PAY TO THE ORDER OF Phil Walden + Associates, Inc. $ 2,355.69

Two thousand three hundred fifty five and 69/100 DOLLARS

THE PEOPLES BANK OF MACON, GA.

PEOPLES BANK
JUN 21 1971

THE ALLMAN BROS. BAND
GENERAL ACCOUNT

FOR mgt fee Duane Allman "Layla" royalties

William H. Perkins

⑆0612⑈1137⑆ 0 11 248 8⑈ ⑈0000235569⑈

ABOVE: Reimbursement to Dickey Betts for car rental expense. *Jack Weston collection*; **MIDDLE:** Twiggs Lyndon paycheck on Brothers Properties, Inc. signed by Charles N. Bignon. *Jack Weston collection;* **BELOW:** Management fee for Duane Allman "Layla" royalties payable to Phil Walden and Associates Inc.

5/30-31

Contract Blank

AMERICAN FEDERATION OF MUSICIANS OF THE UNITED STATES AND CANADA

(HEREIN CALLED "FEDERATION")

PREMIER TALENT ASSOCIATES, INC.

200 WEST 57TH STREET • NEW YORK, NEW YORK

PHONE: PLAZA 7-4300

LOCAL NUMBER 601

MAY 20 1969

THIS CONTRACT for the personal services of musicians, made this 19th day of MAY, 1969, between the undersigned employer (hereinafter called the "employer") and SIX (6) (Including the Leader) musicians (hereinafter called "employees").

WITNESSETH, That the employer hires the employees as musicians severally on the terms and conditions below. The leader represents that the employees already designated have agreed to be bound by said terms and conditions. Each employee yet to be chosen shall be so bound by said terms and conditions upon agreeing to accept his employment. Each employee may enforce this agreement. The employees severally agree to render collectively to the employer services as musicians in the orchestra under the leadership of DUANE ALLMAN-THE ALLMAN BAND as follows:

Name and Address of Place of Engagement BOSTON TEA PARTY BOSTON, MASS.

Date(s) of Employment MAY 30,31, 1969

Hours of Employment TWO (2) FORTY (40) MINUTE SHOWS PER NIGHT BETWEEN THE HOURS OF 8:30 PM AND 1:00 AM. REPORT TIME 6:00 PM.

OPERATOR IS TO PROVIDE A PA SYSTEM. ARTIST BILLED AS EXTRA ADDED ATTRACTION.

Type of Engagement (specify whether dance, stage show, banquet, etc.) SHOW

The employer is hereby given an option to extend this agreement for a period of XXXXXXXXX weeks beyond the original term thereof. Said option can be made effective only by written notice from the employer to the employees, not later than XXXXXXX days prior to the expiration of said original term, that he claims and exercises said option, and a copy of said notice shall be filed with the local in whose jurisdiction the engagement is to be played.

WAGE AGREED UPON $ SEVEN HUNDRED AND FIFTY DOLLARS FLAT ($750.00) (Terms and Amount)

This wage includes expenses agreed to be reimbursed by the employer in accordance with the attached schedule, or a schedule to be furnished the employer on or before the date of engagement.

To be paid DEPOSIT OF $375.00 PAYABLE TO PTA IN CERT. CHECK OR MONEY ORDER IMMEDIATELY. BALANC OF $375.00 PAYABLE TO ARTIST IN CASH ONLY PRIOR TO SHOW NIGHT OF ENGAGEMENT MAY 31, 1969. (Specify when payments are to be made)

Upon request by the American Federation of Musicians of the United States and Canada (herein called the "Federation") or the local in whose jurisdiction the employees shall perform hereunder, the employer either shall make advance payment hereunder or shall post an appropriate bond.

ADDITIONAL TERMS AND CONDITIONS

If any employees have not been chosen upon the signing of this contract, the leader shall, as agent for the employer and under his instructions, hire such persons and any replacements as are required for persons who for any reason do not perform any or all services. The employer shall at all times have complete control over the services of employees under this contract, and the leader shall, as agent of the employer, enforce disciplinary measures for just cause, and carry out instructions as to selections and manner of performance. The agreement of the employees to perform is subject to proven detention by sickness, accidents, or accidents to means of transportation, riots, strikes, epidemics, acts of God, or any other legitimate conditions beyond the control of the employees. On behalf of the employer the leader will distribute the amount received from the employer to the employees, including himself, as indicated on the opposite side of this contract, or in place thereof on separate memorandum supplied to the employer at or before the commencement of the employment hereunder and take and turn over to the employer receipts therefor from each employee, including himself. The amount paid to the leader includes the cost of transportation, which will be reported by the leader to the employer.

All employees covered by this agreement must be members in good standing of the Federation. However, if the employment provided for hereunder is subject to the Labor-Management Relations Act, 1947, all employees, who are members of the Federation when their employment commences hereunder, shall be continued in such employment only so long as they continue such membership in good standing. All other employees covered by this agreement, on or before the thirtieth day following the commencement of their employment, or the effective date of this agreement, whichever is later, shall become and continue to be members in good standing of the Federation. The provisions of this paragraph shall not become effective unless and until permitted by applicable law.

To the extent permitted by applicable law, nothing in this contract shall ever be construed so as to interfere with any duty owing by any employee hereunder to the Federation pursuant to its Constitution, By-laws, Rules, Regulations and Orders.

Any employees who are parties to or affected by this contract are free to cease service hereunder by reason of any strike, ban, unfair list order or requirement of the Federation, and shall be free to accept and engage in other employment of the same or similar character or otherwise, for other employers or persons without any restraint, hindrance, penalty, obligation or liability whatever, any other provisions of this contract to the contrary notwithstanding.

Representatives of the local in whose jurisdiction the employees shall perform hereunder shall have access to the place of performance (except to private residences) for the purpose of conferring with the employees.

The performances to be rendered pursuant to this agreement are not to be recorded, reproduced, or transmitted from the place of performance, in any manner or by any means whatsoever, in the absence of a specific written agreement between the employer and the Federation relating to and permitting such recording, reproduction or transmission.

The employer represents that there does not exist against him, in favor of any member of the Federation, any claim of any kind arising out of musical services rendered for any such employer. No employee will be required to perform any provisions of this contract or to render any services for said employer so long as any such claim is unsatisfied or unpaid, in whole or in part. If the employer breaches this agreement, he shall pay the employees, in addition to damages, 6% interest thereon plus a reasonable attorney's fee.

The employer, in signing this contract himself, or having same signed by a representative, acknowledges his (her or their) authority to do so and hereby assumes liability for the amount stated herein.

To the extent permitted by applicable law, there are incorporated into and made part of this agreement, as though fully set forth herein, all of the By-laws, Rules and Regulations of the Federation and of any local of the Federation in whose jurisdiction services are to be performed hereunder (insofar as they do not conflict with those of the Federation), and the employer acknowledges his responsibility to be fully acquainted, now and for the duration of this contract, with the contents thereof.

NEW ENGLAND CONCERT CORP./DON LAW — Employer's Name

X Don Law — Signature of Employer

53 BERKLEY STREET — Street Address

BOSTON, MASS. — City — State

(617) 338-7026 — Phone

375 5/26

DUANE ALLMAN — Leader's Name — 601 Local No.

X Duane Allman — Signature of Leader

REDWAL MUSIC COMPANY INC.

535 COTTON AVENUE, MACON, GA. — Street Address — City — State

PREMIER TALENT ASSOCIATES, INC. FB:rr — Booking Agent

If this contract is made by a licensed booking agent, there must be inserted on the reverse side of this contract the name, address and telephone number of the collecting agent of the local in whose jurisdiction the engagement is to be performed.

Form B-2a 1-1-59

Personal appearance contract for a very early show at the Boston Tea Party. Duane Allman signature is a facsimile. *Courtesy The Allman Brothers Band Museum at The Big House.*

IT IS AGREED AND UNDERSTOOD THAT AS A PART OF THIS CONTRACT THE EMPLOYEE ASSUMES ALL RESPONSIBILITY FOR ANY AND ALL ADDITIONAL MUSICIANS AS SET FORTH BY THE RULINGS OF THE LOCAL MUSICIANS UNION WITHIN WHOSE JURISDICTION THIS ENGAGEMENT IS PLAYED.

Contract Blank № 0057 CH

AMERICAN FEDERATION OF MUSICIANS OF THE UNITED STATES AND CANADA

(HEREIN CALLED "FEDERATION")

ASSOCIATED BOOKING CORPORATION

919 NORTH MICHIGAN AVENUE, CHICAGO, ILLINOIS 60611

TELEPHONE: 751-2000

THIS CONTRACT for the personal services of musicians on the engagement described below, made this 3RD day of AUGUST 1970, between the undersigned Purchaser of Music (herein called "Employer") and SIX musicians.* (including leader) The musicians are engaged severally on the terms and conditions on the face hereof. The leader represents that the musicians already designated have agreed to be bound by said terms and conditions. Each musician yet to be chosen, upon acceptance, shall be bound by said terms and conditions. Each musician may enforce this agreement. The musicians severally agree to render services under the undersigned leader.

1. Name and Address of Place of Engagement WAREHOUSE, 1820 TCHOUPITOULAS, NEW ORLEANS, LA.

Print Name of Band or Group ALLMAN BROTHERS

2. Date(s), starting and finishing time of engagement SATURDAY, AUGUST 1970 BETW. 9:00 P.M. & 3:00 A.M.

BINDER DEPOSIT RECEIVED
AMOUNT 250
DATE 8/12
BY Wm. Elson
ASSOCIATED BOOKING CORP

3. Type of Engagement (specify whether dance, stage show, banquet, etc.)

4. WAGE AGREED UPON $ 2500 FLAT (Terms and Amount)

This wage includes expenses agreed to be reimbursed by the employer in accordance with the attached schedule, or a schedule to be furnished the Employer on or before the date of engagement.

5. Employer will make payments as follows: 50% DEPOSIT, PAYABLE TO ASSOCIATED BOOKING CORP. BY CASHIER'S OR CERTIFIED CHECK, ON SIGNING OF CONTRACT; BALANCE TO LEADERIN CASH, CASHIER'S OR CERTIFIED CHECK ON NIGHT OF ENGAGEMENT. (Specify when payments are to be made)

Upon request by the Federation or the local in whose jurisdiction the musicians shall perform hereunder, Employer either shall make advance payment hereunder or shall post an appropriate bond.

If the engagement is subject to contribution to the A.F.M. & E.P.W. Pension Welfare Fund, the leader will collect same from the Employer and pay it to the Fund; and the Employer and leader agree to be bound by the Trust Indenture dated October 2, 1959, as amended, relating to services rendered hereunder in the U. S., and by the Agreement and Declaration of Trust dated April 9, 1962, as amended, relating to services rendered hereunder in Canada.

6. The Employer is hereby given an option to extend this agreement for a period of ______ weeks beyond the original term thereof. Said option can be exercised only by written notice from the Employer to the musicians, not later than ______ days prior to the expiration of the original term, and a copy of said notice shall be filed with the Federation local in whose jurisdiction the engagement is to be played.

7. The Employer shall at all times have complete supervision, direction and control over the services of musicians on this engagement and expressly reserves the right to control the manner, means and details of the performance of services by the musicians including the leader as well as the ends to be accomplished. If any musicians have not been chosen upon the signing of this contract, the leader shall, as agent for the Employer and under his instructions, hire such persons and any replacements as are required.

8. In accordance with the Constitution, By-laws, Rules and Regulations of the Federation, the parties will submit every claim, dispute, controversy or difference involving the musical services arising out of or connected with this contract and the engagement covered thereby for determination by the International Executive Board of the Federation or a similar board of an appropriate local thereof and such determination shall be conclusive, final and binding upon the parties.

Additional Terms and Conditions

The leader shall, as agent of the Employer, enforce disciplinary measures for just cause, and carry out instructions as to selections and manner of performance. The agreement of the musicians to perform is subject to proven detention by sickness, accidents, riots, strikes, epidemics, acts of God, or any other legitimate conditions beyond their control. On behalf of the Employer the leader will distribute the amount received from the Employer to the musicians, including himself as indicated on the opposite side of this contract, or in place thereof on separate memorandum supplied to the Employer at or before the commencement of the employment hereunder and take and turn over to the Employer receipts therefor from each musician, including himself. The amount paid to the leader includes the cost of transportation, which will be reported by the leader to the Employer.

All employees covered by this agreement must be members in good standing of the Federation. However, if the employment provided for hereunder is subject to the Labor-Management Relations Act, 1947, all employees who are members of the Federation when their employment commences hereunder shall be continued in such employment only so long as they continue such membership in good standing. All other employees covered by this agreement, on or before the thirtieth day following the commencement of their employment, or the effective date of this agreement, whichever is later, shall become and continue to be members in good standing of the Federation. The provisions of this paragraph shall not become effective unless and until permitted by applicable law.

To the extent permitted by applicable law, nothing in this contract shall ever be construed so as to interfere with any duty owing by any musician performing hereunder to the Federation pursuant to its Constitution, By-laws, Rules, Regulations and Orders.

(Continued on reverse side)

BILL JOHNSON C/O WAREHOUSE X Print Employer's Name	DUANE ALLMAN #601 X Print Leader's Name — Local No.
Bill Johnson Signature of Employer	Duane Allman Signature of Leader
1820 TCHOUPITOULAS Print Street Address	Print Street Address
NEW ORLEANS, LOUISIANA City — State — Zip Code	City — State — Zip Code
Telephone	WILLIAM ELSON Booking Agent

*This contract does not conclusively determine the person liable to report and pay employment taxes and similar employer levies under rulings of the U. S. Internal Revenue Service and of some state agencies.

FORM B-28 10-66

Personal appearance contract at The Warehouse, New Orleans, August 1970. Duane Allman signature is a facsimile. *Courtesy The Allman Brothers Band Museum at The Big House.*

CONTRACT BLANK № 0910 N.Y.

AMERICAN FEDERATION OF MUSICIANS OF THE UNITED STATES AND CANADA
(HEREIN CALLED "FEDERATION")

ASSOCIATED BOOKING CORPORATION

JOE GLASER, President • • **Telephone: HA 1-5200**

445 PARK AVENUE, NEW YORK, N. Y. 10022

LOCAL NUMBER______

THIS CONTRACT for the personal services of musicians on the engagement described below, made this 3rd day of FEBRUARY 19 71 between the undersigned Purchaser of Music (herein called "Employer") and 6 musicians.* (including leader)

The musicians are engaged severally on the terms and conditions on the face hereof. The leader represents that the musicians already designated have agreed to be bound by said terms and conditions. Each musician yet to be chosen, upon acceptance, shall be bound by said terms and conditions. Each musician may enforce this agreement. The musicians severally agree to render services under the undersigned leader.

1. Name and Address of Place of Engagement FILLMORE EAST, 105 SECOND AVE., NEW YORK, N.Y.

   Print Name of Band or Group ALLMAN BROTHERS

2. Date(s), starting and finishing time of engagement MARCH 12th & 13th, 1971

   TWO SHOWS ~~AT~~ BETWEEN 8PM & 2AM

3. Type of Engagement (specify whether dance, stage show, banquet, etc.)______

4. WAGE AGREED UPON $ 5000 (FIVE THOUSAND DOLLARS) NO DEPOSIT. BILLING FOR ARTIST MUST READ "SPECIAL ADDED ATTRACTION". (Terms and Amount)

   This wage includes expenses agreed to be reimbursed by the employer in accordance with the attached schedule, or a schedule to be furnished the Employer on or before the date of engagement.

5. Employer will make payments as follows: all monies DUE ARTIST IN CASH OR CERTIFIED CHECK ~~XXXXXXXXXXXXXXXXXXXXX~~ AT CONCLUSION OF ENGAGEMENT. (Specify when payments are to be made)

Upon request by the Federation or the local in whose jurisdiction the musicians shall perform hereunder, Employer either shall make advance payment hereunder or shall post an appropriate bond.

If the engagement is subject to contribution to the A.F.M. & E.P.W. Pension Welfare Fund, the leader will collect same from the Employer and pay it to the Fund; and the Employer and leader agree to be bound by the Trust Indenture dated October 2, 1959, as amended, relating to services rendered hereunder in the U. S., and by the Agreement and Declaration of Trust dated April 9, 1962, as amended, relating to services rendered hereunder in Canada.

6. The Employer is hereby given an option to extend this agreement for a period of______weeks beyond the original term thereof. Said option can be exercised only by written notice from the Employer to the musicians, not later than______ days prior to the expiration of the original term, and a copy of said notice shall be filed with the Federation local in whose jurisdiction the engagement is to be played.

7. The Employer shall at all times have complete supervision, direction and control over the services of musicians on this engagement and expressly reserves the right to control the manner, means and details of the performance of services by the musicians including the leader as well as the ends to be accomplished. If any musicians have not been chosen upon the signing of this contract, the leader shall, as agent for the Employer and under his instructions, hire such persons and any replacements as are required.

8. In accordance with the Constitution, By-laws, Rules and Regulations of the Federation, the parties will submit every claim, dispute, controversy or difference involving the musical services arising out of or connected with this contract and the engagement covered thereby for determination by the International Executive Board of the Federation or a similar board of an appropriate local thereof and such determination shall be conclusive, final and binding upon the parties.

Additional Terms and Conditions

The leader shall, as agent of the Employer, enforce disciplinary measures for just cause, and carry out instructions as to selections and manner of performance. The agreement of the musicians to perform is subject to proven detention by sickness, accidents, riots, strikes, epidemics, acts of God, or any other legitimate conditions beyond their control. On behalf of the Employer the leader will distribute the amount received from the Employer to the musicians, including himself as indicated on the opposite side of this contract, or in place thereof on separate memorandum supplied to the Employer at or before the commencement of the employment hereunder and take and turn over to the Employer receipts therefor from each musician, including himself. The amount paid to the leader includes the cost of transportation, which will be reported by the leader to the Employer.

All employees covered by this agreement must be members in good standing of the Federation. However, if the employment provided for hereunder is subject to the Labor-Management Relations Act, 1947, all employees who are members of the Federation when their employment commences hereunder shall be continued in such employment only so long as they continue such membership in good standing. All other employees covered by this agreement, on or before the thirtieth day following the commencement of their employment, or the effective date of this agreement, whichever is later, shall become and continue to be members in good standing of the Federation. The provisions of this paragraph shall not become effective unless and until permitted by applicable law.

To the extent permitted by applicable law, nothing in this contract shall ever be construed so as to interfere with any duty owing by any musician performing hereunder to the Federation pursuant to its Constitution, By-laws, Rules, Regulations and Orders.

(Continued on reverse side)

BILL GRAHAM/FILLMORE EAST
Print Employer's Name

X Bill Graham
Signature of Employer

105 SECOND AVENUE
Print Street Address

NEW YORK, NEW YORK 10003
City State Zip Code

Telephone

DUANE ALLMAN #601
Print Leader's Name Local No.

X Duane Allman
Signature of Leader

Print Street Address

City State Zip Code

JOHNNY PODELL-ASSOCIATED BOOKING CORP.
Booking Agent

*This contract does not conclusively determine the person liable to report and pay employment taxes and similar employer levies under rulings of the U. S. Internal Revenue Service and of some state agencies.

FORM B-2B 10-66

SEE RIDER ATTACHED

Personal appearance contract for Fillmore East, March 12-13, 1971. "The Allman Brothers Band at Fillmore East" was recorded at this engagement. Duane Allman signature is a facsimile. *Courtesy The Allman Brothers Band Museum at The Big House, © Wolfgang's Vault. All rights reserved.*

October 11, 1971

ARTIST INFORMATION SHEET — ALLMAN BROTHERS BAND

DATE October 17, 1971

TIME(S) Two (2) shows between 4:30 PM and 8:30 PM

LOCATION Painters Mill Music Fair
10 miles from
Baltimore, Maryland

TELEPHONE

EMPLOYER Steve Talbert, 2814 Erie Street, S.E., Apt. C-44,
Washington, D.C. - Tele. #202-581-2314 or 338-2379

TERMS: GUARANTEE $10,000.00
PERCENTAGE 60% over $22,000.00
GROSS POTENTIAL $16,000.00
DEPOSIT $5,000.00

EMPLOYER TO FURNISH	YES	NO
ORGAN W/2 LESLIES	X	
PUBLIC ADDRESS	X	
LIMOUSINE	X	
TRUCK	X	
OTHER (PLEASE LIST)		

EMPLOYER TO RENT ALLMAN BROTHERS BAND'S SOUND SYSTEM

YES X NO

TERMS $750.00

SPECIAL INSTRUCTIONS Call Steve Talbert at 202-581-2314 before 12 noon or after 7 PM with your flight schedule. He will have someone meet you at the airport with transportation to the location.

Artist information sheet for Painters Mill Music Fair near Baltimore, Maryland, October 17, 1971. *Courtesy The Allman Brothers Band Museum at The Big House.*

"I[illegible] CONTRACT IS NOT SIGNED AND RETURNED WITHIN [illegible] DAYS [illegible] TO ASSOCIATED BOOKING CORPORATION, CO[illegible] WILL BE SUBJECT TO CANCELLATION BY ARTIST."

Cont. Rec'd. 10-4-71

Cont. Ret. 10-11-71 VAMSO

№ 2605 N.Y.

$5,000-

9-30-71

TCY

CONTRACT BLANK

AMERICAN FEDERATION OF MUSICIANS OF THE UNITED STATES AND CANADA

(HEREIN CALLED "FEDERATION")

ASSOCIATED BOOKING CORPORATION

445 PARK AVENUE, NEW YORK, N. Y. 10022 • TELEPHONE: HA 1-5200

LOCAL NUMBER ______

THIS CONTRACT for the personal services of musicians on the engagement described below, made this **24th** day of **September** 19**71**, between the undersigned Purchaser of Music (herein called "Employer") and **6** musicians.* (including leader)

The musicians are engaged severally on the terms and conditions on the face hereof. The leader represents that the musicians already designated have agreed to be bound by said terms and conditions. Each musician yet to be chosen, upon acceptance, shall be bound by said terms and conditions. Each musician may enforce this agreement. The musicians severally agree to render services under the undersigned leader.

1. Name and Address of Place of Engagement **Painters Mill Music Fair, 10 miles from Baltimore, Maryland**

   Print Name of Band or Group **ALLMAN BROS. BAND**

2. Date(s), starting and finishing time of engagement **October 17th, 1971 two shows 4:30PM & 8:30PM**

3. Type of Engagement (specify whether dance, stage show, banquet, etc.) **Artist to receive 100% Headline Billing**

4. WAGE AGREED UPON $ **10,000. (TEN THOUSAND DOLLARS) + 60% over $22,000.**
   (Terms and Amount)

   This wage includes expenses agreed to be reimbursed by the employer in accordance with the attached schedule, or a schedule to be furnished the Employer on or before the date of engagement.

5. Employer will make payments as follows: **$5000. deposit due upon signing of contract. Balance in cash or certified check evening of engagement.**
   (Specify when payments are to be made)

Upon request by the Federation or the local in whose jurisdiction the musicians shall perform hereunder, Employer either shall make advance payment hereunder or shall post an appropriate bond.

If the engagement is subject to contribution to the A.F.M. & E.P.W. Pension Welfare Fund, the leader will collect same from the Employer and pay it to the Fund; and the Employer and leader agree to be bound by the Trust Indenture dated October 2, 1959, as amended, relating to services rendered hereunder in the U. S., and by the Agreement and Declaration of Trust dated April 9, 1962, as amended, relating to services rendered hereunder in Canada.

6. The Employer shall at all times have complete supervision, direction and control over the services of musicians on this engagement and expressly reserves the right to control the manner, means and details of the performance of services by the musicians including the leader as well as the ends to be accomplished. If any musicians have not been chosen upon the signing of this contract, the leader shall, as agent for the Employer and under his instructions, hire such persons and any replacements as are required.

7. In accordance with the Constitution, By-laws, Rules and Regulations of the Federation, the parties will submit every claim, dispute, controversy or difference involving the musical services arising out of or connected with this contract and the engagement covered thereby for determination by the International Executive Board of the Federation or a similar board of an appropriate local thereof and such determination shall be conclusive, final and binding upon the parties.

Additional Terms and Conditions

The leader shall, as agent of the Employer, enforce disciplinary measures for just cause, and carry out instructions as to selections and manner of performance. The agreement of the musicians to perform is subject to proven detention by sickness, accidents, riots, strikes, epidemics, acts of God, or any other legitimate conditions beyond their control. On behalf of the Employer the leader will distribute the amount received from the Employer to the musicians, including himself as indicated on the opposite side of this contract, or in place thereof on separate memorandum supplied to the Employer at or before the commencement of the employment hereunder and take and turn over to the Employer receipts therefor from each musician, including himself. The amount paid to the leader includes the cost of transportation, which will be reported by the leader to the Employer.

All employees covered by this agreement must be members in good standing of the Federation. However, if the employment provided for hereunder is subject to the Labor-Management Relations Act, 1947, all employees who are members of the Federation when their employment commences hereunder shall be continued in such employment only so long as they continue such membership in good standing. All other employees covered by this agreement, on or before the thirtieth day following the commencement of their employment, or the effective date of this agreement, whichever is later, shall become and continue to be members in good standing of the Federation. The provisions of this paragraph shall not become effective unless and until permitted by applicable law.

To the extent permitted by applicable law, nothing in this contract shall ever be construed so as to interfere with any duty owing by any musician performing hereunder to the Federation pursuant to its Constitution, By-laws, Rules, Regulations and Orders.

(Continued on reverse side)

Employer	Leader
Mr. Steve Talbert	Duane Allman #601
Print Employer's Name	Print Leader's Name / Local No.
X Copy Given to Willie Perkins Signed by	X
Signature of Employer	Signature of Leader
2814 Erie Street, S.E. Apt. C-44 PROMOTER	
Print Street Address	Print Street Address
Washington, D.C.	
City / State / Zip Code	City / State / Zip Code
202-581-2314 store 338-2379	BILL HALL-Associated Booking Corporation
Telephone	Booking Agent

*This contract does not conclusively determine the person liable to report and pay employment taxes and similar employer levies under rulings of the U. S. Internal Revenue Service and of some state agencies.

FORM B-2B REV. 7-70 44

"THIS CONTRACT IS SUBJECT TO SIGNATURE OF ALL PARTIES CONCERNED."

Personal appearance contract Painters Mills Music Fair, October 17, 1971. This was Duane Allman's final appearance with The Allman Brothers Band. Duane Allman's signature is a facsimile. *Courtesy The Allman Brothers Band Museum at The Big House.*

PARAGON AGENCY 1019 WALNUT STREET • MACON, GEORGIA 31208 • TEL. 912/742-3

July 18, 1973

Mr. Willie Perkins
535 Cotton Avenue
Macon, Georgia

Dear: Willie

YOUR COMPLETED CONTRACT IS ATTACHED

Artist: Allman Brothers Band

Date: July 28, 1973

Terms: $117,500.00 flat

Deposit: $ 37,500.00 (received)

Pick-up: $ 80,000.00

Location: Watkins Glen Grand Prix Race Track
Watkins, New York

Employer: Shelly Finkel
Country Concerts, Inc.
655 Madison Avenue
New York, New York

phones: 212 758-6211

Rehearsal time:

Time of performance: One 150 minute show beginning at 10pm.

Special Information: Set up time is 12 noon July 26.

Pat Page

Pat Page
Contract Department
Paragon Agency

pp

Enclosure

41,875
4) 167,500

29
4) 117,500
8
37

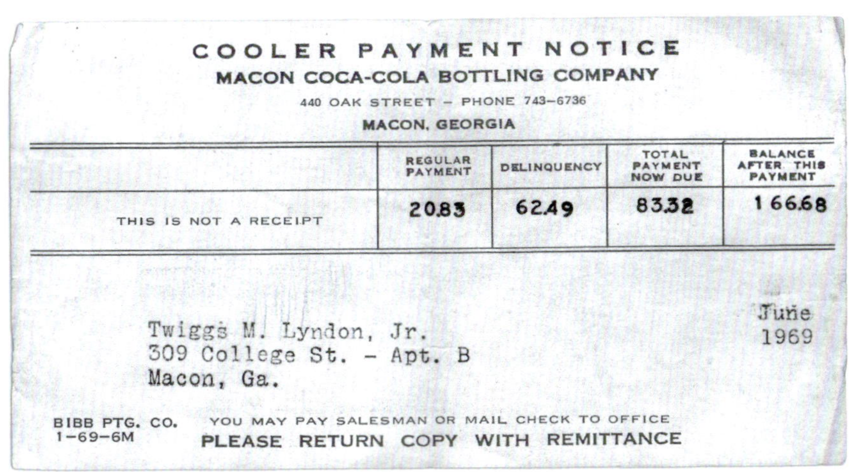

COOLER PAYMENT NOTICE
MACON COCA-COLA BOTTLING COMPANY
440 OAK STREET – PHONE 743–6736
MACON, GEORGIA

	REGULAR PAYMENT	DELINQUENCY	TOTAL PAYMENT NOW DUE	BALANCE AFTER THIS PAYMENT
THIS IS NOT A RECEIPT	20.83	62.49	83.32	166.68

Twiggs M. Lyndon, Jr.
309 College St. – Apt. B
Macon, Ga.

June
1969

BIBB PTG. CO.
1–69–6M

YOU MAY PAY SALESMAN OR MAIL CHECK TO OFFICE
PLEASE RETURN COPY WITH REMITTANCE

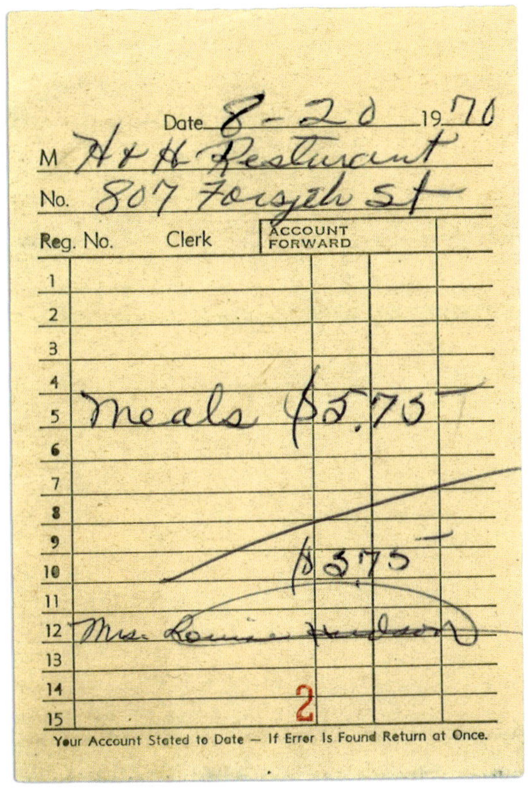

Date 8-20 1970
M H & H Restaurant
No. 807 Forsyth St

Reg. No. Clerk ACCOUNT FORWARD

5 Meals $5.75

$3.75

12 Mrs. Louise Hudson

2

Your Account Stated to Date — If Error Is Found Return at Once.

ABOVE: Payment on Coca-Cola vending machine located in original College Street band apartment. This was used to dispense beer. *Courtesy The Allman Brothers Band Museum at The Big House;* **BELOW:** Cash receipt for band meal at H & H Restaurant signed by Mama Louise Hudson. *Courtesy The Allman Brothers Band Museum at The Big House;* **OPPOSITE:** Personal appearance cover letter for Watkins Glen, New York, July 28, 1973. The Allman Brothers Band management negotiated approximately $86,000 in additional payments above the stated contract fee of $117,500. *Jack Weston collection.*

Blockout – photos

PARAGON AGENCY

Booking Slip

DATE ISSUED 3/30/71

DATE DUE

EMPLOYEE(S) ABB

LEADER

TO CONSIST OF

DATE(S) OF ENGAGEMENT April 5 & 6

TERMS

DEPOSIT

HOURS OF EMPLOYMENT

REHEARSAL

LOCATION Photos -

STREET

CITY/STATE Macon, Ga.

TELEPHONE(S)

CONTRACT NO.

AFM ☐ AGVA ☐ OTHER ☐

ANOTHER AGENCY ☐

EMPLOYER(S)

STREET

CITY/STATE

TELEPHONES

COMMISSIONS DUE OFFICE

COMMISSIONS DUE EMPLOYEE

CHARGES

SEND PUBLICITY WITH CONTRACT ☐

HOLD PUBLICITY FOR CONTRACT ☐

SPECIAL INSTRUCTIONS:

Jim Marshall

notify - Willie have entire band available in Macon -

Advisement to Willie Perkins to have band available for Jim Marshall photo shoot of "At Fillmore East" LP cover in Macon on April 5th and 6th, 1971. Handwriting on bottom right hand corner is Phil Walden's. *Courtesy The Allman Brothers Band Museum at The Big House;* **OPPOSITE:** Ledger sheet showing personal appearance income, circa 1970. *Courtesy The Allman Brothers Band Museum at The Big House.*

Month	Day	Description				Balance
						55249 00
10	16	Georgetown, Ky	1250 00	→		56499 00
10	17	Spartanburg, S.C.	1496 00	→		57995 00
10	23	Stoneybrook, N.Y.			1250 00	
10	24	Ashland, Va			3000 00	
10	25	Buck County, Pa			2500 00	64745 00
10	27	Deposit on ABC date - Bucks County	250 00			64495 00
10	28	Western Carolina, N.C.			2250 00	
10	30	Nashville, Tenn			3500 00	
10	31	Atlanta, Ga			1700 00	
11	1	Charlotte, N.C.			1000 00	72945 00
11	6	New Orleans, La Tulane			3000 00	
11	7	✓ ✓ ✓ Warehouse			1250 00	77195 00
11	14	Detroit, Mich			3500 00	80695 00
11	18	Athens, Ga			3000 00	83695 00
11	21	Boston, Mass			3000 00	86695 00
11	22	New Paltz, N.Y.			3500 00	90195 00
11	25	B'ham, Ala			1550 00	
11	26	Sarasota, Fla			2770 00	
11	28	St. Pete, Fla			3000 00	97515 00
12	3	Greenville, N.C.			2250 00	
12	4	Columbia, S.C.			3800 00	
12	5	Fayetteville, N.C.			1125 00	104690 00
12	10	New Haven, Conn.			1800 00	
12	12	New York, NY			4000 00	
12	13	Washington, D.C.			1250 00	
12	14	Boston, Mass			1000 00	
12	15	Ringe, N.H.			750 00	
12	18	L.A., Cal			2700 00	
12	19	San Diego			1000 00	117190 00
12	29	Orlando			2500 00	
12	31	New Orleans			2000 00	121690 00
	✓	Advance from Walden-RE Duane			335 47	122025 47
	✓		122025 47			-0-

Income

Personal Appearance - Pickup

Month	Day	Place	Amount	Monthly Total	Running Total
1	7	Statesboro, Ga	1775 00		
	8	Charlotte, N.C.	4000 00		
	9	Knoxville, Tenn.	2000 00		7775 0
	15	Boone, N.C.	4000 00		
	16	Atlanta, Ga.	2713 00		
	17	Pittsburgh, Pa	3750 00		18238 0
	23	Port Chester, N.Y	4000 00		
	24	Hampton, Va	1500 00		23738 0
	26	Cincinnati, Ohio	2000 00		25738 0
	31	San Francisco, Cal	2700 00	28438 00	28438 00
2	3	Los Angeles, Cal	1350 00		
	4	Delaware, Ohio	1750 00		
	5	Philadelphia, Pa	1750 00		
	8	Troy, Alabama	3500 00		36788 0
2	10	High Point, N.C.	1550 00		
	12	Greenville, S.C.	4000 00		
	13	Charleston, S.C.	4000 00		46338 00
	20	Burlington, Vt	3500 00		
	✓	Rindge, N.H	1750 00		51588 00
	22	as of 2/15 Ft. Lauderdale, Fla	4000 00		
	✓	✓ ✓ ✓ Albany, Ga	3500 00		59088 00
	23	Steubenville, Ohio	1000 00		
	24	Greenville, Pa	3000 00		
	25	Cleveland, Ohio	2500 00		
	27	Detroit, Mich	2000 00	39150 00	67588 00
3	13	NYC	6250 00		
	14	Selden, N.Y	2000 00		75838 00
	20	New Orleans, La	2000 00		
	21	La Fayette, ✓	1500 00		
	25	St Paul, Minn	1750 00		
	27	Asbury Park, N.J.	2500 00		
	27	(as of 3/24) Tuscaloosa, Ala.	4500 00	20500 00	88088 00
4	2	Madison, N.J.	2500 00		
	3	Bethlehem, Pa.	2000 00		92588 00
	7	Miami, Fla.	2000 00		
	8	W. Palm Beach, Fla	4000 00		
	9	Macon, Ga	3193 00		
	10	Sarasota, Fla.	1750 00		
	11	Jacksonville, Fla.	3059 00		106590 00
	14	Decatur, Ala	2000 00		
	16	Columbia, S.C.	2000 00		
	17	Charlotte, N.C.	2460 00		
	18	Harrisburg, Pa	4000 00		117050 00
	22	Murphreesboro, Tenn	4750 00		
	23	Greensboro, N.C.	4000 00		
	25	University Park, Pa	5000 00		130800 00
	27	Island Park, N.Y.	1500 00		132300 00

	Initials	Date
Prepared By		
Approved By		

Direct Expense 71

	Jan	Feb	March	Apr	May	June	July	Aug	Sept	Oct	Nov	Dec
Freight	32521	66692	61425	28613	105536	149737	94842	4275	262063	212869	4615	
Rehearsal	5000		45000		9300						10000	
Equip.	190961	867495	51179	457767	41635	302925	249918	231087	97165	45530 ~~28185~~	89066	
Union	18720	4935	8103	1599	7544	1356	10639	2744	4121	6105	(891)	
Insurance						7646	7646		7646	18362	42816	
Gas & Oil	30793	55548	133312	52085	94079	34732	76083	59563	68857	36540	-	
Emp. Tr. [illegible]									40000	167500	82500	
Medical										250000		
Acct	7500	7500	7500	7500	11500	7500	111500 ~~1445~~	7500	7500	7500	7500	
Camper	11340	5817	(400)					4830				
Hotel & Mo	217919	238717	203649	225756	255618	381642	349668	314413	250739	463495	165872	
Air	273350	158445	1224693	1034096	807757	942950	866828	722708	1844019	1375998	206140	
Car & Truck Rent	129134	105756	378134	219249	390810	222194	284712	218084 ~~[illegible]~~	204277	182510	156714	240553
Misc	37871	52358	35528	76053	66261	13906	90474	116775	74872	68816	84006	105164
Repairs Equip	111053	6460	2730	36152	28107	15156	7547	26781	60889	34937	7688	6345
Van	0 ~~8886~~	0 ~~6886~~	4837 ~~14423~~	15117 ~~23703~~	28964 ~~59540~~	0 ~~8586~~	6107 ~~14693~~	0 ~~8586~~	1007 ~~9593~~	4853 ~~13439~~	0	0
Other ~~Ad val tax~~	485	10985	485	485	15485	485	485	485	485	485	485	53755
Casual Labor	23400	38000	69500	37733	121710	-0-	95000	-0-	111400	35500	115000 ~~65000~~	105582
Cab	39580	19700	10600	23300	15845	17135	24050	12160	29855	22380	-0-	19355 ~~[illegible]~~
Legal	-	-	200000	-	30000	-	-	-	-	-	-	81161
Tel & Tel	-	-	-	6241	3400	5000	1624	1343	380	2493	—	—
Adv & PR												114459

Ledger of band expenses, 1971. *Courtesy The Allman Brothers Band Museum at The Big House;* **OPPOSITE:** Ledger sheet showing personal appearance income, circa 1971. *Courtesy The Allman Brothers Band Museum at The Big House.*

CHAPTER
11
MISCELLANEOUS
Wipe the Windows : Check the Oil ·
Allman Brothers

ABOVE: Bronze sculpture of Duane Allman cast by Ellen Hopkins in 1969. A limited edition of 26 were cast in the early 1990's and sold to collectors. © *Ellen Hopkins;* **OPPOSITE:** Cape worn by Berry Oakley in early band publicity photos taken at Rosehill Cemetery, Macon, Georgia. *Courtesy Linda Oakley, Richard Price photo.*

WILLIE PERKINS

In conclusion, there are some interesting one of a kind and small volume collectibles that the average fan will rarely be able to obtain. However, they should not go without mention. These include Berry Oakley's cape seen in an early promotional photo of the band. It is still intact and owned by his widow Linda. Other examples of band members' stage wear and street clothing are held by family members and in public and private collections. Guitar straps, belts, and belt buckles are also of interest. A small number of belt buckles were produced for commercial sales to the general public. Various fans and friends have created one of a kind drawings, paintings, and even a statuette.

Glass slide bottles actually used by Duane Allman while performing are extremely rare and very difficult to authenticate. I can attest that one was included in his coffin prior to his memorial service. Gold and platinum record sales awards were produced in small quantities for band, crew, employees, and family members. They also went to management, booking agents, record company personnel, and various VIPs.

Finally, among several municipal and state awards, The Allman Brothers Band actually received the key to the City of Jacksonville, Florida. Duane and I joked that it was probably the back door key. It resides in The Big House Museum in Macon, Georgia.

JACK WESTON

Longtime band friend Ellen Hopkins created a small statue of Duane Allman in wax in early August 1969. In 1974 Johnny Sandlin asked Ellen if it still existed and she then made the first casting in bronze. Per Ellen Hopkins' recollection, twenty six copies have been made since the first bronze was cast.

I own an original piece of artwork that was created as a line drawing by the Wonder Graphics team of James Flournoy Holmes and W. David Powell in late 1971 or early 1972. This was originally used as an advertisement in *Billboard Magazine* by Capricorn Records to promote The Allman Brothers Band. In 2005 I commissioned W. David Powell to rework the original line art and add watercolors to it. David added colors utilizing the same set of Dr. Martin's watercolors he used for the "Eat A Peach" gatefold art. He did make some minor changes to the drawing itself before he added the watercolor.

Two separate, one-of-a-kind, leather made artifacts that come to mind are the guitar straps that Duane Allman used from 1969 until his death in October of 1971. The first of these was a leather guitar strap with a 5-inch brass girth ring. The ring was manufactured by The North and Judd Co. and was stamped with an anchor symbol. This strap was created and hand tooled by Ted "Zebo" Starker in 1969 at his leather repair shop in Sarasota, Florida. Duane used this strap during some of his session work at Muscle Shoals, Alabama, as well as in 1969 and the first part of 1970 with The Allman Brothers Band. Dixie Meadows recalls having a hand tooled guitar strap made for Duane by Phil Thomas at Jim Cole's leather shop in Atlanta that Duane used in 1970 and 1971. It had a long mountain range, cactus, sage brush, dragons, birds, a moon, stars, and other images hand tooled on it. This strap has come to be known as Duane's Mountain Guitar Strap and is currently on exhibit at the Hard Rock Cafe in Nashville, Tennessee. Another interesting leather artifact is Willie Perkins' mushroom belt. Willie wore this belt in the mid 1970's. Gregg Allman also had an identical mushroom belt at that time.

As some of the artifacts in the miscellaneous category are made of leather, these need special care. If leather artifacts are no longer being used, the use of leather conditioners is not necessary. If they are to be occasionally used I use Lexol leather conditioner as well as Pecard leather dressing. What is most important is keeping the humidity level as close as possible to 40 percent and also limiting ultraviolet light exposure. Maintaining these conditions will help to reduce the chance of leather artifacts cracking over time. The conservation of miscellaneous paper items has already been covered in this book. I store all my miscellaneous fabric artifacts in a cedar closet to prevent moth damage.

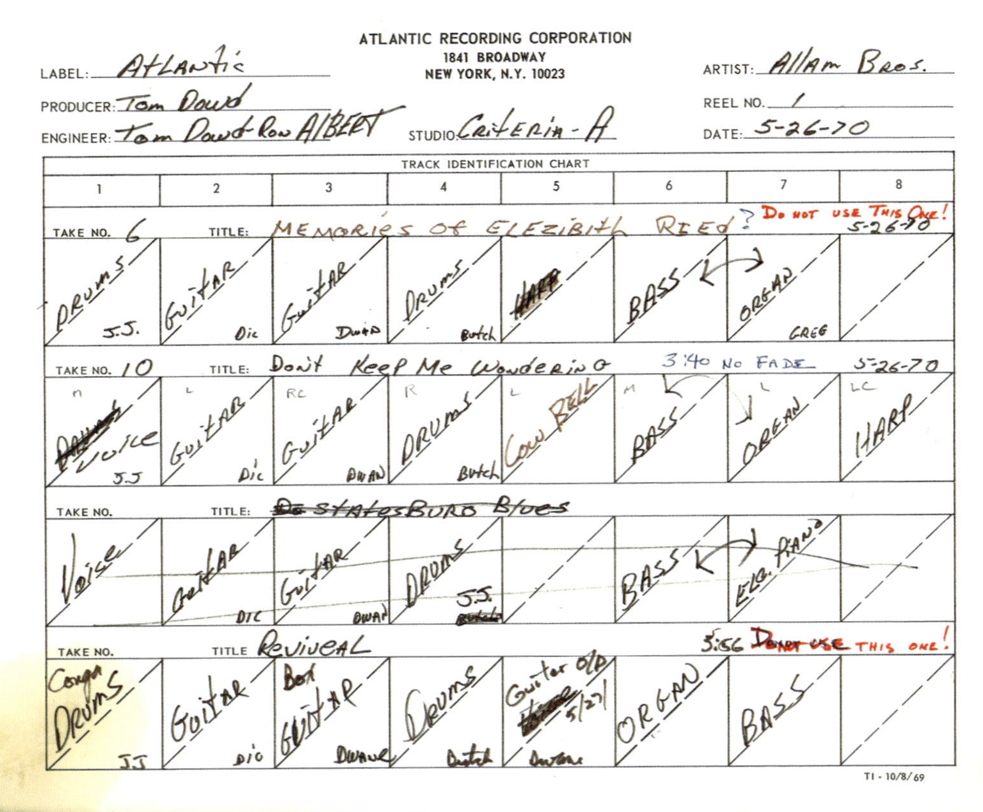

ATLANTIC RECORDING CORPORATION
1841 BROADWAY
NEW YORK, N.Y. 10023

LABEL: AtLAntic
PRODUCER: Tom Dowd
ENGINEER: Tom Dowd Ron ALBERT
STUDIO: CRiteRia - A
ARTIST: AllAm BRoS.
REEL NO. 1
DATE: 5-26-70

TRACK IDENTIFICATION CHART

TAKE NO. 6 TITLE: MEMORIES OF ELEZIBITH RIED ? Do NOT USE THIS ONE! 5-26-70

1	2	3	4	5	6	7	8
DRUMS J.J.	GUITAR Dic	GUITAR DwAn	DRUMS Butch	~~HARP~~	BASS	ORGAN GREG	

TAKE NO. 10 TITLE: Don't Keep Me WondeRinG 3:40 No FADE 5-26-70

1	2	3	4	5	6	7	8
~~Drums~~ Voice J.J	GUITAR Dic	GUITAR DwAn	DRUMS Butch	Cow BELL	BASS	ORGAN	HARP

TAKE NO. TITLE: ~~StatesBoro Blues~~

1	2	3	4	5	6	7	8
Voice	GuitAR Dic	GUITAR DwAn	DRUMS J.J. ~~Butch~~		BASS	ELE. PIANO	

TAKE NO. TITLE RevivAL 5:56 ~~Do not use~~ THIS ONE!

1	2	3	4	5	6	7	8
Conga DRUMS J.J	GUITAR Dic	Box GUITAR Dwane	DRUMS Butch	Guitar O/D 5/27 Dwane	ORGAN	BASS	

TI - 10/8/69

Tracking sheet from Criteria Studios Miami, Florida, dated May 26, 1970 from "Idlewild South" recording sessions.

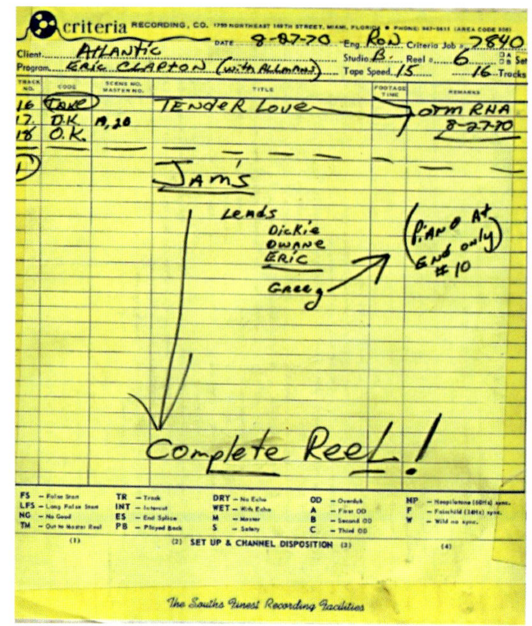

criteria RECORDING, CO.

Client: Atlantic — Date: 8-27-70 — Eng.: Ron — Criteria Job: 2840

Program: Eric Clapton (with Allmans) — Studio: B — Reel: 6 — Tape Speed: 15 — 16 Tracks

Track No.	Code	Scene No. Master No.	Title	Footage Time	Remarks
16	Take		Tender Love		OTM RHA 8-27-70
17	O.K.	19, 20			
18	O.K.				
1			Jams		

Leads: Dickie, Duane, Eric, Gregg (Piano at end only #10)

Complete Reel!

FS – False Start; LFS – Long False Start; NG – No Good; TM – Out to Master Reel; TR – Track; INT – Intercut; ES – End Splice; PB – Played Back; DRY – No Echo; WET – With Echo; M – Master; S – Safety; OD – Overdub; A – First OD; B – Second OD; C – Third OD

SET UP & CHANNEL DISPOSITION

The Souths Finest Recording Facilities

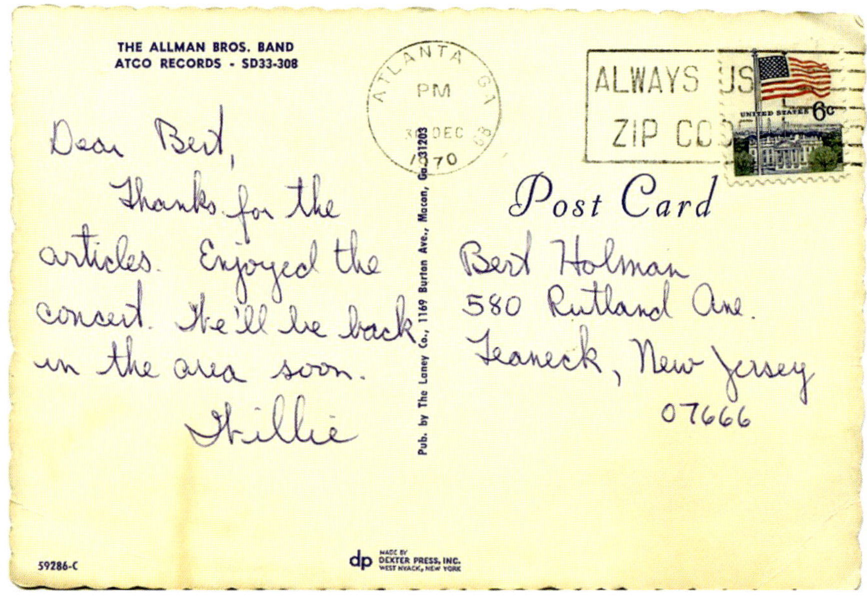

THE ALLMAN BROS. BAND
ATCO RECORDS - SD33-308

Dear Bert,
Thanks for the articles. Enjoyed the concert. We'll be back in the area soon.
Willie

ATLANTA GA PM 30 DEC 1970

ALWAYS USE ZIP CODE

Post Card

Bert Holman
580 Rutland Ave.
Teaneck, New Jersey
07666

Pub. by The Laney Co., 1169 Burton Ave., Macon, Ga. 31203

59286-C

dp MADE BY DEXTER PRESS, INC. WEST NYACK, NEW YORK

ABOVE: Recording tape box from Criteria Studios, Miami, Florida, August 27, 1970, for "Layla" sessions. Contains jams with Dickey Betts, Duane Allman, and Eric Clapton. *Courtesy Eric Clapton;* **BELOW:** Postcard from Willie Perkins to Bert Holman dated December 30, 1970. At that time Bert was a student and concert promoter at American University in Washington, D.C. Bert later became the personal manager of The Allman Brothers Band. **OPPOSITE:** Tracking sheet from Criteria Studios, Miami, Florida, 1971 "Eat A Peach" sessions.

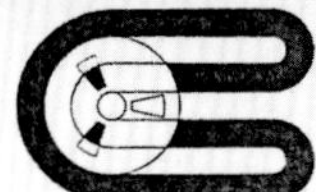

criteria recording studios 1755 NE 149 ST/MIAMI FLORIDA 33161/305 947-5611

TAKE NO. TITLE Blue Sky

	1	2	3	4	5	6	7	8
	~~Vocal~~ GOOD VOCAL FOR [illegible]	Vocal LEAD DEC. 2, 1971	HARMONY VOCAL DEC 2, 1971	Organ	Guitar Dickie	Guitar Duane	Drums Jay	
EQ	EIGHT BARS							
PAN	AFTER INST.	0/0	0/0	0/-10	-5/0	0/-5	0/-10	0/-6
LIM	ONLY!!							
CUE	DEC 2, 1971							

	9	10	11	12	13	14	15	16
	Drums Butch		Bass Direct	Bass Mike	Electric Piano	Box #1 O/D Duane	Box #2 O/D Duane	[illegible] O/D TAMB. Drum repair
EQ								TURN INTO
PAN	-6/0	-10/0	0/0	0/0	-10/0	0/-30	-20/0	3rd VERSE
LIM								[illegible] BEFORE
CUE								TAMBORINE [illegible]

TAKE NO. TITLE ~~Road to Calico~~ (STAND BACK)

	1	2	3	4	5	6	7	8
	Vocal 2nd Line Only	Vocal		Organ	Guitar Dickie	Guitar Duane	Drums Jay	
EQ								
PAN	0/0	0/0		0/-10	0/-5	-5/0	0/-∞	0/-4
LIM								
CUE								

	9	10	11	12	13	14	15	16
	Drums Butch		Bass Direct	Bass Mike	Electric Piano	Percusion	Guitar Double O/D Dickie	Guitar Double O/D Duane
EQ							INTRO ONLY	
PAN	0/0	-∞/0	0/0	0/0	-10/0	-7/0	0/-5	-5/0
LIM								
CUE								

Label Engineer Reel No.

Producer Artist Date

"Little Martha"

criteria recording studios 1755 NE 149 ST/MIAMI FLORIDA 33161/305 947-5611

TAKE NO. TITLE Little Martha

	1	2	3	4	5	6	7	8
	Dickie Acoustic		Duane Acoustic		Bass			
EQ								
PAN								
LIM								
CUE								

	9	10	11	12	13	14	15	16
EQ								
PAN								
LIM								
CUE								

TAKE NO. TITLE

	1	2	3	4	5	6	7	8
EQ								

A Key to the City of Jacksonville, Florida, presented by the Mayor to Duane Allman and the band at a concert in 1970 or 1971. *Courtesy The Allman Brothers Band Museum at The Big House, Kirk West photo.*

B An example of a Coricidin brand cold remedy bottle of the type used by Duane Allman to play slide guitar. *Courtesy The Allman Brothers Band Museum at The Big House, Kirk West photo.*

C Styrofoam cup embossed with mushroom logo. These cups were used at all band concerts. *Jack Weston collection.*

OPPOSITE: The original The Allman Brothers Band mushroom design on cover of band publicity folder. *Jack Weston collection.*

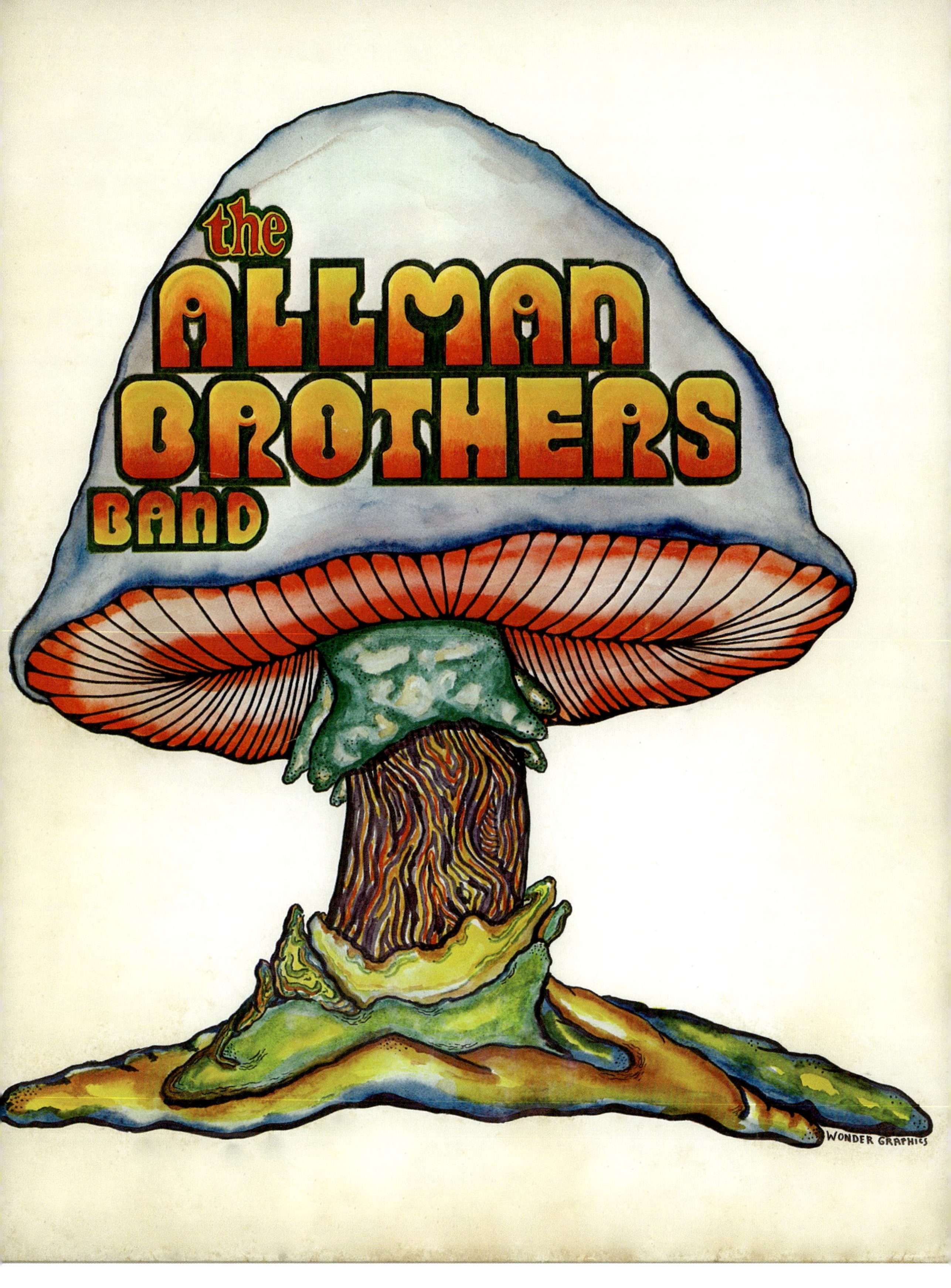
the
ALLMAN
BROTHERS
BAND
WONDER GRAPHICS

Handmade leather jacket presented to Duane Allman by a fan and friend, now on display at The Allman Brothers Band Museum at The Big House. Duane later gave this jacket to Willie Perkins. *Courtesy The Allman Brothers Band Museum at The Big House, Jim Burt photo.*

ERIE COUN[illegible]

ERIE COUNTY JAIL
10 DELAWARE AVENUE
BUFFALO, NEW YORK 14202

MAY 4 1970
Censored By
Badge No.

FROM:
Inmate's Full Name
Twiggs Miller Lyndon, Jr.
Cell No. J2 Date: May 4, 1970
(WRITE ON RULED LINES ONLY)

TO:
NAME: Phil Walden
STREET: 535 Cotton Avenue
City: Macon,
State: Georgia 31201

Dear Phil,
Considering the situation everything is really going OK. I have been treated very well here (Good Food, hot, three times a day, private room, T.V., and everything is nice and clean). All of the guards and officials are very polite, no harresment, and all in all, I am very comfortable. I Don't exactly Know how I got so much help so fast, but I feel sure that you must have been responsible, and I really want to thank you. I sincerally appreciate you and everybody else standing behind me in a time like this. I couldn't really ask you to stand in front, now, could I? Seriously It is really a load off my mind to Know that I have so many friends. Thank's Everybody!
Bunky if there is any way possible for you and Ollie to help make it happen, I sure would like to see the High Hope Project be a sucess. If its not possible, I Understand. If there is any Information you need Please drop me a line!

(JAIL RULES)

VISITORS: Inmates are allowed one visit on Tuesdays and Thursdays (including Holidays) for 10 minutes. Hours are from 9:15 to 11:30 AM and 1:15 to 3:15
ONLY IMMEDIATE FAMILY ALLOWED TO VISIT INMATES:
LETTERS TO INMATES: Address in care of the Erie County Jail. Write plainly and make sure postage is sufficient. Family and business matters only may be discussed in letters. Do not mail personal checks or cash. All letters received and sent are censored and objectional material removed. Only two (2) sheets will be accepted.
GIFTS TO INMATES: No papers, tobacco in any form, candy or edibles of anykind will be accepted and packages are carefully examined.

JAILOR OF ERIE COUNTY

Personal letter from Twiggs Lyndon to Allman Brothers Band manager Phil Walden, dated May 4, 1970. *Courtesy Twiggs Lyndon family.*

ABOVE: Original, flat-ring guitar strap owned and used by Duane Allman in the early years. This strap was custom made by Ted "Zebo" Starker at his Sarasota, Florida, shop in 1969. The brass ring was manufactured by North and Judd. *Courtesy Cathy Brantley, Richard Price photo;* **BELOW/OPPOSITE:** Duane Allman's "mountain" guitar strap (details on opposite page). This strap was custom made in Atlanta, Georgia, as a gift from Dixie Meadows to Duane Allman. The strap is currently on display at The Hard Rock Cafe in Nashville, Tennessee. *Courtesy Hard Rock Cafe International (USA), Inc., John Lee Montgomery III photo.*

Volume Four, Number Forty-Five

Copyright/Atlanta Cooperative News Project/1971

November 8, 1971

20¢

25¢ outside Atlanta

The Great Speckled Bird

duane allman — oct. 30, 1971

Duane Allman memorial edition of Atlanta underground newspaper *The Great Speckled Bird*, November 1971. *Jack Weston collection, Carter Tomassi photo.*

ABOVE: Early 1970's business card for Brothers Properties, Inc., the corporate entity of The Allman Brothers Band. *Courtesy Willie Perkins, Jack Weston collection;* **BELOW:** Original cardboard mobile for in-store promotion of Capricorn Records release of "Wipe the Windows - Check the Oil - Dollar Gas." *Jack Weston collection.*

ABOVE: "Win, Lose, or Draw" belt buckle. *Jack Weston collection;* **BELOW:** Custom made mushroom belt originally owned by Willie Perkins. Gregg Allman and "Scooter" Herring also had identical belts. *Jack Weston collection.*

ABOVE: "Eat A Peach" belt buckle. *Jack Weston collection*; **BELOW:** Mid-70's belt buckle, likely a bootleg item. *Jack Weston collection.*

Platinum record award presented to Gregg Allman to commemorate the sale of more than one million copies of the album "Eat A Peach." *Courtesy The Allman Brothers Band Museum at The Big House, Chip Jones Photography.*

Platinum record award presented to Phil Walden and Associates to commemorate the sale of more than one million copies of the album "At Fillmore East." *Jack Weston collection, Chip Jones Photography.*

Jack Weston personally commissioned this artwork to be colorized from an original black and white line drawing used in an early 1970's Capricorn Records advertisement. *Courtesy W. David Powell and James Flournoy Holmes, Jack Weston collection.*

ACKNOWLEDGMENTS

Exhaustive efforts were made by the authors to be accurate and to obtain permissions from rights holders where necessary. We sincerely regret any inadvertent errors or omissions and they may be corrected in future editions.

We would also like to thank the following for their assistance and support:

The Allman Brothers Band / Galadrielle Allman
The Allman Brothers Band Museum at The Big House / Mike Bagwell,
Ron Blair / Bonnie Bramlett / Cathy Brantley / Richard Brent,
Eric Clapton / Alex Cooley / Connie Butler / Eric Custer,
E. J. Devokaitis / Grant Feichtmeir / Shelly Finkel / The Grateful Dead,
John Griffin / Hard Rock Cafe / Alex Hodges / Bert Holman
James Flournoy Holmes / Ellen Hopkins / Chip Jones / Jim Koplik
Scot LaMar / Don Law / Skip Littlewood / Kenny Loggins
Andy Lyndon / John Lyndon / Skoots Lyndon / the late Twiggs Lyndon
Larry Magid / Brian McBride / Dixie Meadows / Bill Meriwether
John Lee Montgomery III / Nico Narum / Linda Oakley / Stephen Paley
Alan Paul / Michael Pierce / W. David Powell / Richard Price,
Anathalee Sandlin / Johnny Sandlin / Rebecca Roby
The Rock and Roll Hall of Fame / Amalie R. Rothschild / Bill Sagan
Savage Amps / David Schless / the late Curt Souza / Sidney Smith
the late Ted "Zebo" Starker / Skip Simmons / Carter Tomassi
Derek Trucks / Sandy Bluesky Wabegijig / Jenni West / Kirk West
Leslie West / Bobby Whitlock / Steve Winwood / Jared Wright
and Otto Zielke

“AND THE ROAD GOES ON FOREVER”